Ramón "Tianguis" Pérez

TRANSLATED BY DICK J. REAVIS

Arte Publico Press
Houston
Texas
1991

This book is made possible by a grant from the National Endowment for the Arts, a federal agency.

Recovering the past, creating the future

Arte Público Press
University of Houston
452 Cullen Performance Hall
Houston, Texas 77204-2004

Cover design by Mark Piñón
Original painting by Adán Hernández:
"La media luna" Copyright © 1989

Pérez, Ramón ("Tianguis")
    [Diario de un mojado. English]
    · Diary of an Undocumented Immigrant / Ramón "Tianguis" Pérez;
translated by Dick J. Reavis.
    p. cm.
    Translation of Diario de un mojado.
    ISBN 1-55885-032-5
    1. Pérez, Ramón ("Tianguis")   2. Alien labor, Mexican—United
States—Biography.   I. Title.
HD8081.M6P4713 1991
323.6'092-dc20   91-7869
    [B]   CIP

⊛ The paper used in this publication meets the requirements of the American National Standard for Information Sciences—Permanence of Paper for Printed Library Materials, ANSI Z39.48-1984.

    6 7 8 9 0 1   13 12 11 10 9 8 7 6 5

For my fellow *mojados.*

Diary of an Undocumented Immigrant

From Oaxaca to the Rio Grande

CROSSING THE BORDER

My luggage is a small vinyl suitcase that holds one change of clothes. It's a bag for a person who has left home for a couple of days, but I don't know when I'll return to my village. Bigger than my bag is the mountain of goodbyes I'm carrying. My mother was so touched that she made the sign of the cross over me with a wax candle that is probably burning upon the altar of the church right now. My father, more used to goodbyes than mothers, told me, "Stay on your toes, boy," while he was giving me a hug. My brothers told me to send them postcards from the places I will find myself. Last night, my friends and I made the rounds, drinking.

It's about eleven o'clock in the morning and I'm walking the eight kilometers that separate my village from the highway that snakes over the peak of the mountain range. There's a dirt road that comes from it to my village, but there isn't always a passing truck on which to catch a ride. But this time, I'd rather walk the distance anyway.

The summer sun isn't extreme, but the exercise makes me sweat. Before leaving, I spent more than an hour beneath the showerhead and then changed into the clothes that my mother had ironed. It took more time for me to shower and change than it has for me to get bathed in sweat. But at least it made my mother happy to see me leave clean and in fresh clothes.

If my ancestors had known that the international highway was going to pass just eight kilometers from the village, maybe they would have decided to establish the village farther up, but I can't blame them. They probably had their own reasons for putting the village midway down the mountains, and I myself have learned that the closer land is to the peaks, the less fertile it is. Higher up, the cold is more intense and the peak is covered with snow. Beneath us, the heat is sultry, while in our village, the climate is mild. Now that I think about it, my ancestors were entirely right, and I'm sure that before digging the groundwork for the foundation of the village's first house, they set it precisely at the midpoint of the mountain.

Halfway between the village and the highway is a hill from which you can view the panorama of the village, and I rest there for a minute. In the middle of the thick forest of pines and oaks and other trees, a mild breeze comes up to me, fresh and comforting, but the rays of the sun don't let it become cold. There below, encircling the village, the cornfields have begun to dry, a sign that within two months people will bring in the harvest. The cornfields are a coffee-colored scene, and their sameness gives the impression of a giant blanket whose stitches sway with the wind. Below are the tin roofs of the village, shining beneath the sun, and in the middle, the church of thick, whitewashed walls with a dome on one side and a bell tower on the other. Next to the church I can see the top of the big ash tree that is probably as old as the village. The tree has been pruned to avoid accidents, they say, ever since the days when the electric lines came. From here, I can also see a white haze over the houses, smoke that comes from kitchen hearths. But by afternoon, gusts of wind will blow it far away.

Sure, I know, everybody loves his hometown and the region where he was born. But I've been in tropical climates where people have to resort to a fan to create a little breeze, and in those places, the greeting among people is, "How hot it is!" and the response is, "Yes, man, how hot!" I guess I'm lucky not to know how the Eskimos say good morning. Here, you don't need a fan and much less do you need a heater in the summertime.

Of course, not everything about my village is so temperate. It, too, has suffered inclemency. Several little creeks run around the village, and three of them run right through it, and right now the creeks are running too deep. The old people say that back in 1945 it rained day and night for forty days and people thought that the end of the world was coming. The rains were so plentiful that they deepened the course of the creeks, which before, had run almost level to the ground. The dirt kept mixing with the water until the land was cut with gullies that got deeper as the canals of the creeks grew wider. Those creeks grew and grew until it was impossible to cross them. The mudholes broke open and they, too, became like springs and they added their water to the swollen creeks. The waters carried trees, rocks and houses with them, everything that they found in their path. In the village, food grew scarce. The little that was in the stores didn't last long, and people began eating their chickens and the pigs that they were keeping to fatten. The roads became impassable. Cows drowned. The harvest was lost. One of my townsmen, worried because he had left his cattle tied-up outside of the village, tried to cross one of the creeks by floating on a log. But the water wasn't only running swiftly, it was also full of mud, branches and the trunks of trees. He was drowned before he got to the middle of the creek. The townspeople say that after the rains, or the flood, his family tried to find his body to bury it, but all they encountered was his hat, which was stuck in the branches of a bush. Those people who stayed afterwards are still in town, and they will stay even if another flood comes, because water can't dig as deep as the roots of our Zapotec village.

HEADED NORTH

In another half hour of walking, I'll arrive at the highway where I'll catch a bus to take me to Oaxaca City. From there another bus will carry me to Mexico City, then yet another one will take me to Nuevo Laredo, on the border. My plan is to go to the United States as a *mojado*, or wetback.

It didn't take a lot of thinking for me to decide to make this trip. It was a matter of following the tradition of the village. One could even say that we're a village of wetbacks. A lot of people, nearly the majority, have gone, come back, and returned to the country to the north; almost all of them have held in their fingers the famous green bills that have jokingly been called "green cards"—immigrant cards—for generations. For several decades, Macuiltianguis—that's the name of my village—has been an emigrant village, and our people have spread out like the roots of a tree under the earth, looking for sustenance. My people have had to emigrate to survive. First, they went to Oaxaca City, then to Mexico City, and for the past thirty years up to the present, the compass has always pointed towards the United States.

My townsmen have been crossing the border since the forties, when the rumor of the *bracero* program reached our village, about ten years before the highway came through. The news of the *bracero* program was brought to us by our itinerant merchants, men who went from town to town, buying the products of the region: corn, beans, coffee, *achiote*, *mescal*, eggs, fabric dye, and fountain pen ink. The merchants carried these items on the backs of animals, or sometimes, on their own backs, until they reached the city of Oaxaca, about a three days walk from home. On their return trips, they brought manufactured products, like farm tools, cooking utensils, coarse cotton cloth, ready-made clothing and shoes, candies and so on. They sold their goods from house to house, town to town. One of them came with the news that there were possibilities of work in the United States as a *bracero*, and the news passed from mouth to mouth until everyone had heard it.

12

To see if the rumor was true, a merchant and two others went to the U.S. embassy in Mexico City. The only document the embassy required them to provide was a copy of their birth certificates, for which they came back to the village. On their return to Mexico City, they were contracted to work in California.

From the day of their departure, the whole town followed the fate of those adventurers with great interest. After a little while, the first letters to their families arrived. The closest kinsmen asked what news the letters contained, and from them the news spread to the rest of the villagers. Afterwards, checks with postal money orders arrived, and their families went to Oaxaca City to cash them. The mens' return home, some six months later, was a big event because when they came into town they were seen carrying large boxes of foreign goods, mainly clothing.

Their experience inspired others, but not all of them had the same good fortune. Some were contracted for only short periods, because each time there were more people waiting for the same opportunity at the contractors' offices. That's when some men smelled a good business; the men called *coyotes*, the forerunners of today's alien smugglers. They were men who, for a sum of money, intervened in the Mexican offices where contracts were given to make sure that their clients were included in the list of men chosen.

The contractual system came to an end with the *bracero* program, in the mid-sixties, but ending the program didn't end Mexican desires to cross the border. People had learned that in the United States one could earn a wage much higher than the standard Mexican wage, even if to do it one had to suffer privations, like absence from one's family. So when the *bracero* program ended, the *coyotes* kept working on their own. They looked for employers in the U.S. and supplied them with workers illegally.

I, too, joined the emigrant stream. For a year I worked in Mexico City as a nightwatchman in a parking garage. I earned the minimum wage and could barely pay living expenses. A lot of the time I had to resort to severe diets and other limitations, just to pay rent on the apartment where I lived, so that one day I wouldn't come home and find that the owner had put my belongings outside.

After that year, I quit as night watchman and came back home to work at my father's side in the little carpentry shop that supplies the village with simple items of furniture. During the years when I worked at carpentry, I noticed that going to the U.S. was a routine of village people. People went so often that it was like they were visiting a nearby city. I'd seen them leave and come home as changed people. The trips erased for a while the lines that the sun, the wind and the dust put in a peasant's skin. People came home with good haircuts, good clothes, and most of all, they brought dollars in their pockets. In the *cantinas* they paid for beers without worrying much about the tab. When the alcohol rose to their heads, they'd begin saying words in English. It was natural for me to want to try my luck at earning dollars, and maybe earn enough to improve the machinery in our little carpentry shop.

During my infancy, I always heard people say "*Estadu*," because that's the way that "*Estado*," or state, is pronounced in Zapotec, our language. Later on, people simply said "*El Norte*," "The North," when referring to the United States. Today when somebody says "I'm going to *Los*," everybody understands that he's referring to Los Angeles, California, the most common destination of us villagers.

But I'm not going to Los Angeles, at least not now. This time, I want to try my luck in the state of Texas, specifically, in Houston, where a friend of mine has been living for several years. He's lent me money for the trip.

THE RUNNER

The waiting room at the bus station in Nuevo Laredo is spacious and well-lit. It is full of people walking in different directions with bags in their hands. Some are just coming in, some are leaving. Some are in line to buy tickets, and others are seated in the terminal, nervous or bored. A tattered beggar has laid some cardboard sheets on the floor of one corner and he's sitting there, chewing on a piece of hardened bread, his supper before retiring for the night. The waiting room clock marks nine p.m. My traveling companions seem content to have arrived, but I notice them yawning from tiredness; the trip took fourteen hours. Some of them try to comb their disheveled hair and others rub their red eyes. On seeing them, I decide that I probably have the same appearance.

Disoriented, I take a seat in the waiting room, hoping to shake off my own sleepiness. I know what I should do next. I should go out onto the street, take a taxi to a hotel, rest a while and then look for a *coyote*, or alien smuggler. Before setting out, I take my belongings and head towards the restroom, thinking that a stream of cold water across my face will help me wake up.

With the first steps I take towards the restroom, a dark-skinned guy comes up alongside me. He's short and thin and he's dressed in a t-shirt and jeans. He greets me familiarly, with a handshake. After looking him up and down, I'm sure that I've never seen him before. I give him a stern look, but he smiles broadly at me, anyway.

"Where are you coming from, my friend?" he says.

"From Mexico City," I answer.

"From Mexico City!" he exclaims. "Well, man, we're neighbors! I, too, am from Mexico City."

He reaches out and shakes my hand again.

I already know the type from memory. It's not the first time that a stranger has come up to me, saying almost the same things. I am waiting for him to tell me that he had suffered such and such instances of bad luck and that he had a relative in danger of dying

15

and that he had to go to the relative's bedside and that, though it pained him to be without resources, he at least felt encouraged to have come upon a townsman who could give him a little money. But instead of saying that, the stranger keeps walking at my side.

"Where are you headed?" he asks.

I keep silent and without breaking my pace I give him an inquisitorial look, trying to figure out why in the devil's name he's trying to insert himself into my affairs. Still smiling and talking, he repeats his question, as if I hadn't heard him the first time.

"To Houston, I hope to arrive in Houston, with luck, and I'm going to have to find a *coyote*," I tell him, because, given his insistence, I suspect that he might know something about the border-crossing business.

"Are you looking for a particular *coyote*? Has somebody recommended one?" he asks with growing interest.

"I don't know any and nobody has recommended one, and in just a minute, I've got to begin looking for one."

"Well, you're in luck, friend!" he exclaims, adopting the mien of a happy man, content to have brought good news. "You don't have to keep looking, because I"—he points to his chest with the index finger of his right hand—"work for the best and the heaviest *coyote* in Nuevo Laredo. ... The heaviest," he repeats, emphasizing every syllable as if pronouncing the word really was a task of heavy labor.

After entering the restroom, I go up to the urinal, an earthen-colored, tiled wall with a narrow drainage canal at its foot. I start making water and my stranger friend does the same.

"A Mexican never pisses alone," he says, recalling an old saying.

"Right now we have forty *chivos* ready to leave in the early morning, and they're going precisely to Houston, your same destination, my friend."

I'd later learn that they call us *chivos*, or goats, because of the odor we exude from lack of bathing facilities and clean clothing. I am surprised by the ease with which I've run into at least the assistant of a *coyote*, but I don't show much interest in knowing more about his work. After urinating, I go to a sink, open a faucet, and with cupped hands I wet my face a time or two. My friend follows me to the sink and plants himself nearby, without pausing in his praises of his *coyote* boss.

"How much is it going to cost me?" I ask, without raising my head from the sink.

"Four hundred and fifty dollars, plus four thousand pesos for the boat," he answers.

"Good, if that's all, paying will be no problem."

"Very good!," he exclaims with a triumphant gesture. "Well, my friend, in less than eighteen hours you'll be in Houston."

"That's even better," I say, holding back my happiness.

Then my unexpected friend takes a couple of steps and thinking, he says to me, "There's something missing. We've got to be sure that you'll pay that amount or that it will be paid for you."

"That's no problem. You will be paid when I get to Houston."

I'm carrying the money, but my distrust tells me that I shouldn't let the stranger know. The money is a loan of $650. I've got $100 in my billfold. The other $550, in bills of $50 each, is sewn into the lining of my jean jacket.

"Oh," he says, answering himself, "you've got a relative who is going to pay for you in Houston. It's incredible how everybody has relatives in the United States."

Without my asking, he has told me what my answer should be, should anyone else question me about money. I'll say that my friend will pay in Houston. Nobody will know that I'm carrying the money myself.

"It's not really a relative that I've got, it's a friend," I say, to get the story rolling.

"You should give us the phone number of your friend so that we can make sure that he really knows you and will pay for you."

"That's no problem," I tell him, just for the moment. The telephone number could be a problem because my friend has asked me to use his name only if it's urgent. He also asked me not to carry his telephone number and address with me. I have complied with his requests. I memorized his name and address. The only problem I can foresee will be to find a way to tell him that if the *coyotes* call, he should promise to pay for me.

The friendly stranger doesn't stop trying to convince me that his boss is a powerful man. He says that his boss is invulnerable because he has paid-off the police.

"On top of that," the stranger says, "he treats the *chivos* better than anyone else, because he gives them a house to stay in while they're waiting. The other *coyotes* put people out in the brush without jackets and a lot of times, without food. Not to mention the way he treats me," the guy adds. "He doesn't pinch pennies when we're out drinking."

I'm more interested in what he says about payment than in his endless homage to his boss.

"Do I have to pay for the boat every time it crosses the Rio Grande, or only to cross without incident?" I ask him, while I'm drying my face with the sleeve of my jacket.

"Oh, no!" he says, as if scolding himself for having forgotten an important detail. "If *La Migra* catches you ten times, we'll put you across ten times for the same money. And what's more"—his face brightens as if with surprise—"my boss is right here in the station. Come on, I'll introduce you!"

We go walking towards the station's cafeteria, and the stranger who says he's my townsman points towards a group of three men seated at a table, each one in front of a can of beer.

"Do you see that dude who's wearing the cowboy hat? Well, that's Juan Serna, he's my boss," he tells me, with the pride and arrogance of someone who has introduced a Pancho Villa. "All you have to do is say that you're a client of Juan Serna, and the police will leave you alone, because—let me tell you—if you go outside to the street right now and you take a taxi at the next block, or if you catch a city bus, the Judicial Police will grab you—and forget it!— they'll let you go on the next corner, with empty pockets. They'll rip-off your change, man. But if you tell them that you're with Juan Serna, they themselves will take you to the house where we keep the *chivos*."

"Wait for me here," he says when we've come within a prudent distance of the table where the three men are chatting. "I'm going to tell the boss that you're going to Houston."

He walks towards the table and speaks to the man named Juan Serna, then looks towards me. With a movement of his hand, he tells me to come nearer.

Juan Serna is dressed in an orange, nylon t-shirt with black lettering on its frontside that says, "Roberto Duran #1." He's dark-complexioned with somewhat fine facial features. His eyes seem very deep in their sockets. He's clean-shaven, with a wispy moustache. Beneath his eyes are the wrinkles of a man bordering on fifty. Several tattoos adorn both arms, most prominent among them is the head of Jesus, dripping blood from his crown of thorns. Juan Serna doesn't waste good humor like his assistant. He remains rigid, as if preoccupied with other affairs. He leans forward a little, supporting his body upon the table with his forearms, his hands clasped around a can of beer. He makes no gesture and gives no greeting when his assistant introduces us, only a rapid look, a look as indifferent as if he'd been handed the next can of beer. His two companions are seated in front of him, and they're saying something that I can't hear. My "townsman" stands, waiting expectantly at Juan Serna's side.

"Where are you going?," Serna says to me in a northern accent and in a voice so dry that it sounds like he's formed his question not in his mouth, but in his throat.

"To Houston."

"Do you have someone to pay for you there?"

"My friend who lives in Houston."

"So should I take him?" my townsman says.

Juan Serna gives his consent by nodding at my townsman, but he nods without moving a single muscle of his face. I follow my townsman, with the impression that behind us Juan Serna is still nodding, like the branch of a tree that sways involuntarily after somebody has pulled on it.

Outside the bus station, the townsman leads me to a station wagon. He and I get into its back seat.

"We have to wait until the driver arrives," he says.

From the floor of the vehicle he picks up a six-pack and hands me a can.

"What's your name?," he asks.

"Martín," I say, just to give a name.

"My name is Juan, just like the boss," he says without my having asked him. "And I won't give you my last name because I don't know you, but I'll gladly tell you my nickname. You can call me Xochimilco, just like everybody here does."

While I sip on my beer, Xochimilco drinks one, then another, and a third, chatting all the while.

He says that he was a taco vendor in the Xochimilco district of Mexico City, and that was the reason for his nickname. The taco business had been a good one because his boss had lent him a car to go to places where people amassed, like soccer games. But things went bad when the boss had to sell his car. Xochimiloco says that he found himself first without work, and then without money. He found it necessary to ask a friend for a loan of five thousand pesos.

Xochimilco began to worry when his friend put twice the amount he'd asked for into his hands. He accepted only after making long declarations of gratitude. A month later, that same friend came to his house in a luxurious new car. "When from the doors to my house I saw him pull up," Xochimilco says, "I immediately thought about the loan he'd made me, and I was really relieved when he said that I should forget about it, because I still didn't have anything in my pockets."

His friend told him that if he was still in need, he'd help him get past his troubles, on the condition that he cooperate with the friend's plans. When Xochimilco asked in what way he could help, his friend laid a .38 calibre automatic pistol in his hands. Xochimilco didn't know what to say, but he looked with fascination upon the gun given to him.

"At first, it frightened me," Xochimilco tells me, "because I'd never shot a pistol, much less shot at a human being."

"Who said that you're going to kill anybody?" his friend said when Xochimilco expressed reservations. Xochimilco decided to trust his friend in the hopes that he, too, would someday have a car like his. His friend and another guy had planned a hold-up.

"Five hundred thousand pesos for only one simple hold-up!" Xochimilco bragged after a long swig of beer. "Your nerves make you tremble after the first job."

But Xochimilco's money troubles were finished. After the first job came others. The gang's biggest and last hit came after they had gotten to know the son of the owner of a slaughterhouse. The son was firmly resolved to rob his father, who he said was swimming in money but was so cheap that he wouldn't spend a cent, not even on himself. And the son, who knew his father's routine, conspired with Xochimilco and his friends. The four of them went into the father's office just as he was counting bills on his desk with the company safe open. When he realized that he was being robbed, the father reached for a pistol that he kept in his desk, but the bandits all opened fire, even the son. They made off with four million pesos; Xochimilco's cut came to half a million. Time passed and investigations began. When the son was arrested, Xochimilco decided to flee to *El Norte.*

"I had enough money to pay a *coyote*," Xochimilco says, with a slight and fleeting expression of nostalgia. After two attempts, he managed to reach Houston but he only stayed a month because one night, on leaving a beer joint drunk, the police stopped him and turned him over to agents of *La Migra*, the Immigration and Naturalization Service. A couple of days later, he was taken back to Nuevo Laredo. Now with only ten thousand pesos to his name, he could neither return to Mexico City nor cross the border again. He asked the man who is now his boss to give him a job.

"And here you have me," Xochimilco says. "I'm a runner. They call us that because we're always running behind guys that we suspect are headed to the United States."

I ask him how much he earns. He says that of the four thousand pesos that I'll pay for the boat, two thousand are for him. "I make that much for every *chivo* I take to Juan Serna's house."

"I imagine that you're not exactly poor," I tell him.

"Well, okay," he says, teasing, "I've made enough to have money, but I don't have it saved, because ... well, what good is money? Huh, my friend?" His eyes open into an interrogatory look as he leans closer to me. "To spend it! If not, what good is it?"

His job, he says, pays him different sums on different days, especially because he isn't the only runner.

"You can ask for 'Shell,' for the 'Mosquito,' or for the 'Dog.' Anybody can tell you about them, they're in the same business as me. Today I can pick up ten clients and tomorrow, none. That's the way this job is."

Xochimilco interrupts his explanations to point out a car that has parked in front of the terminal.

"That car without license plates belongs to the Judicial Police, and I can assure you that it won't be long before Juan Serna comes out to talk to them."

Just as he said, a minute later Juan Serna comes out of the terminal and walks directly up to the car without plates.

"Do you see it! Look at that!" Xochimilco exclaims. "What I tell you is no lie. That son-of-a-bitch is well-connected."

A few minutes later, a middle-aged man sits down in front of the steering wheel of the car where Xochimilco and I are waiting. Without saying a word, he starts the motor and we pull off.

"That idiot," Xochimilco says, pointing to the driver, "is the one they call 'Shell.' "

The car passes over paved streets, and for a few minutes, bumps down dirt streets full of chugholes. Meanwhile, I'm thinking that my circumstances are like those of a fugitive. To avoid being stopped by the police I have to keep company with thieves and maybe murderers, who, oddly enough, enjoy police protection. If the police stop me, I could argue that I'm a Mexican citizen, with a right to be in any part of the Republic, and I could point out that the police don't have the right to suppress my rights unless I'm committing a crime. To be a wetback, to go into the United States illegally, isn't a crime that's mentioned in our Constitution, but whether or not it is, it's not important. Here, he who's going to be a wetback, if he has money, will have trouble with the police, and if he doesn't have money, he'll have even more trouble. The idea that the police watch over the social order is an old tale that's true only in my village, where we name the policemen from among our own townsmen. If they find you drunk, they're likely to drag you home. If you deserve a punishment, the worst that can happen to you is a night in jail.

THE HOUSE OF JUAN SERNA

We pass down streets that the constant movement of vehicles has turned into a sauce the color of the earth, and pocked with holes of stagnant water. The water that has flooded these streets comes from a broken water line, Xochimilco tells me as we come to a stop on a residential street and get out of the car. He leads me to a dark patio.

"Be careful where you walk," Xochimilco says. "Don't step on those who are sleeping."

"More people?" says a voice from among the bundles stretched out on the floor.

"That one is new," says a voice that also comes from the earth, close to my feet, which are looking for space in which to step. "Did you at least clean your shoes before coming in? You're going to get the carpet dirty," the voice says.

I grope as I advance, getting used to the dark. I come upon a stack of four concrete building blocks and sit down on them. Then I light a cigarette.

"You've got cigarettes?" says one of the dark bundles and, without waiting for my response, asks me to give him one.

Seconds later, others join in, making the same request, and I have to throw the package away, empty. I'd opened it only a short time before.

The patio is about five yards by five yards in size, though it is not exactly square. Walls enclose it on three sides. Two of them are the walls of a habitation, to judge by the window in one wall and the door in the other. The third wall marks the property limits. The other side of the patio is bound by an old wooden fence whose pickets seem tired of standing in the same position, and have leaned against one another in the direction of the ground. Only a single strand of wire holds them up. At the foot of this fence, on the inside, a small area is marked-off by brick laid in the ground, where somebody apparently tried to make a little flower garden. Only a few stalks have remained, and it's impossible to tell what kind of plants they represent. The patio is roofless; over our heads there's a dark blue sky, starry and clean, but without a moon. Far off I can see the glow of a streetlight, but the patio is shrouded in semi-darkness.

Before spotting a place in which to stretch my legs, I count thirty-five *chivos*, including me. I can't sleep, so I walk from one end of the block to the other. Then I sit down on a pile of sand beneath a street light. One of my new companions comes over, still rubbing his eyes.

"Don't you feel bad smoking alone?" he says.

I hand him a cigarette from a newly opened pack.

"When did you get in?" he asks me.

"About an hour ago," I say.

He tells me that he's headed for Dallas and that they'll charge $600 for the trip. His clothes need washing. The collar of his shirt shines with the grease and grime of several days. His black hair is dirty and uncombed. His teeth are yellow and his eyes are red, and they express boredom and tiredness, just like his voice.

"They told me that we'll leave about dawn," I tell him.

Dawn is about half an hour away.

A slight smile crosses his lips. He looks at me jokingly, and then goes back to the patio and lies down again. I wait a few minutes, and then I return, too.

A bluish light comes on in one of the rooms at the side of the house, and then I hear the sound of a television set. Through a window in one wall, I see it glowing. After a few seconds, I hear the voice of a woman scolding a crying child. The child has interrupted her viewing. Between my back and the ground there's only a dirty rug, but fortunately, the night is warm and only a jacket is needed to keep warm. Despite its open-air setting, the patio smells like a human warehouse. The smell is a mixture of body and foot odor— foot odor because people have put their shoes beneath their heads, to use as pillows. There's also the smell of a basin used for washing clothes by the family that lives in the house. But the *chivos* don't seem to be bothered, if only because most of them are sound asleep. The loud snoring of some men stops as soon as they're in a deep slumber. Some of them turn over, lying sometimes on their backs, sometimes on their stomachs, sometimes on their sides. A few stand up and walk towards the street, but after a while, they return to their sleeping spots. Later, when the television goes off, the little window, which looked like a sinister phosphorescent eye becomes a black spot along the wall. The voice of the woman tells someone to go to sleep, and then all is silent again.

Sunrise comes without any news. Though I am tired and sleepless from the bus trip, I have stayed awake most of the night, waiting for someone to tell us at any moment that we should be on our way, like Xochimilco had said we'd be. But day breaks and no one has called us for anything.

A few men rise lazily with the sun. They slowly pick themselves up, then make their way to the street in front of the house, where they sit down on the sand pile. Two big cars sit on wooden blocks, one on each side of the street. Four or five men are sleeping inside each of them. Opposite the house of Juan Serna is a house of weatherbeaten wood, behind a fence of the same material, and on one side, a cement patio that looks like a mechanic's shop. Two cars with Texas license tags are parked there. The motor of one of them has been taken apart. The other car's transmission lies on the ground. Further back is a sty in which four medium-sized pigs are resting.

About thirty yards from that there's a big garbage dump whose stench will get stronger in the morning with the heat. Parts of the dump are like lakes of sour water on which an infinitude of trash is floating. Their waters are nearly red-colored in some ponds and green in others.

The sun has warmed the patio at Juan Serna's house and now the flies buzz around its dirty carpet like a revolving black cloud. Two fat women about thirty years of age, sloppy and tired, carrying deep baskets filled with dirty clothes, walk towards the washing basin that stands on one corner of the patio.

"Those who came in last night!" shouts a man they call Shell. "Come to the office!"

Six of us go up to the door that Shell points out, the same from which the two women had come from. The door squeaks when we open it.

The office is a small room, almost wholly occupied by a double bed that hasn't been made. On one side is a small wooden table upon which a telephone, alarm clock and several empty beer cans are stacked. The beer cans have been crushed.

Juan Serna comes out of the adjoining room. He's shod in sandals, his hair is disheveled, and deep circles surround his eyes. He looks as if he is having a hard time keeping his eyelids open.

"Did you guys come in last night?" he asks. "Did they tell you how much you should pay? Well, come by one at a time. The rest of you, wait your turn outside."

When my turn comes, Juan Serna goes to great lengths to tell me what Xochimilco has already told me.

"Who will answer for you in Houston?"

"My friend."

"You'd better give me his telephone number so that I can talk to him to make sure that he knows you and will pay for you."

"There's no problem. My friend will pay as soon as I get to Houston."

"Your word doesn't work" he says.

I assure him that my friend will pay.

"You're not the first one to come to me with such tales," he says. "I don't have to give you any explanation, but I'll tell you that I've sent people who have sworn to me on their mothers and grandmothers and have begged me until I believed them and, at the end of it all, they say that they don't have any money, and there's no point in bringing them back here."

"I promise you that my friend will pay. He doesn't want me to use his telephone number because he doesn't want any problems."

"Well, there are problems, all right! The problem is that we can't take you that way. This isn't any game," he says with irritation. "You get your friend to give you his telephone number and when you've got it, let me know so that I can check it. And if you want to stay here meanwhile, you'd better pay the four thousand pesos for the boat."

I hand the four thousand pesos to Juan Serna. I know the telephone number by heart, but I've held back because if Serna were to call now, my friend might not know that he should say yes, and I can't explain without Serna and the others learning that I've actually got the money with me.

"If you're going downtown," one of my companions tells me when I say that I plan to go, "be very careful about the cops. They're real sons-of-bitches."

"But I was told," I explain, "that if we just say that we're with Juan Serna, the police will leave us alone."

"Who are you going to believe?" he tells me, lamenting over my innocence. "These guys and the cops, they're all thieves. If you're not careful, they'll search you and rob you."

"I can see now that there will always be babes to fool," he continues. "They tell those things to everybody, so that you'll want to go with them. They told me the same thing, and here I am. I've been waiting for ten days, and the only difference is, I already know how these things work. For ten years I've been living as a wet, and every year I go back to visit my family in Guanajuato. Yesterday early in the morning they sent about twenty guys, and I think it must have gone well, because none of them has come back. But there are always people waiting here."

"So when will we leave?," I ask him.

"Here you've got to be patient, boy. Some guys have had the good luck to leave as soon as they arrived, but that doesn't happen often. Here you have to be patient. Later on you'll find out that some of us have been waiting for up to thirty days. Some of the others have crossed, but *La Migra* has caught them and they've come back. That's the way it is. They come back and they return to try again until they finally make it."

"I'm going to go see if I can light a fire so that we can boil water for coffee," he says, stirring. "But first, give me another cigarette."

When the sun has fully risen, the men who slept in the cars get up. They walk from side to side of the street, then look for places to sit down. On the patio everybody rises. Everyone looks dirty and bored.

I decide not to go downtown, hoping that I can work something out here.

I watch as several of the *chivos* come in with bags of bread, crackers and soft drinks.

"What time do they hand out the food?" I ask one of them.

He looks at me, and then at his companions as if to say, "Look at this idiot."

"Only God knows," he says. "It could be now, or in a little while, or not until tonight. That's why, if you're hungry, you'd better do like us."

By noon, about fifty of us are waiting at Juan Serna's house. Most of them are from the northern part of Mexico, although there are a few of us from the south, from Oaxaca, Morelos, Puebla, Chiapas, Tabasco and Mexico City. Everybody is headed for a different place, some to Houston, Dallas, Florida, and Chicago.

At noon, the sun reaches its peak and forces us all to spread out, looking for shade. To kill the boredom, some of us chat, and others play cards.

One of us says that he has crossed at Nuevo Laredo before, for the same price of four thousand pesos, but with a different *coyote*, who put him and several others on the north bank of the Rio Grande and left them in the brush for several days with a ration of only one sandwich a day. In desperation some of them tried to go north alone, but they were caught by *La Migra* when they tried to hitch rides or board freight trains.

"And you have to be careful," another man says. "You can't cross the river by yourself, and there are thieves on both banks, and you're lucky if they only rob you. Sometimes they drown people, too."

"And if you die in the River," yet another adds, "who is going to reclaim your body? Nobody. So that means that you'll be buried in a common grave, just like a dog."

Another says, "The good thing about the *coyotes* is that they can't collect from a dead man, so they have to protect us against all kinds of dangers."

Not far away, two men lean over the trunk of the dismantled car. A sheet of paper is spread out before them. They tell me that they're peasants, owners of some land. Apparently, they're trying to make some calculations about their land, but they can't come to an agreement about the square of one hundred. One maintains that it is a thousand square meters, the other says that it's ten thousand. After they decide that they can't agree, each one goes a separate way. I hear one of them saying that only God knows, that ten thousand is too big a number to be the square of one hundred.

About three o'clock we hear someone on the patio shouting in a hoarse voice. Some men hurry and others don't, but we all go to receive our share of the food that's ready. Once there, everybody jostles, trying to be first in line. Two fat women are standing in the entrance of the room that's called the office. One of them holds a huge spoon in her hand, submerging it from time to time into a big aluminum pot. The other is in charge of the various and brightly-colored plastic plates. Dozens of hands reach out to her. The fare is potatoes mixed with beans. Outside, a boy of about twelve hands packets of tortillas to those who've already gotten their plates. Some men sit down and put the plates on their laps; others sit on their haunches, with their plates on the ground.

Later that afternoon, Xochimilco arrives with more people, among them two women, one of them with a two-year-old child in her arms.

Shell comes out of the office and everybody encircles him, asking when we'll leave. "Today before sunup," he says, "but only twenty-four will go."

A black van with smoked windshields pulls up in front of the house. Two muscular men are inside. The passenger's arm hangs out the window, like a massive tree trunk. The men have well-trimmed and carefully combed, short haircuts, and their heads almost touch the roof of the van. They wait, staring forward. Not a muscle of their faces twitches. They're expressionless, as if they were mechanical parts of the van. Juan Serna comes out of the office and goes up to them. He leans with both forearms on the door of the driver's side. The van's occupants look at him from the corners of their eyes, barely turning their heads. The driver's lips move rapidly as he mutters something. Juan Serna goes back into the office and returns, seconds later, with a packet that he hands to the driver. Without exchanging a word or a gesture, the men in the van drive off.

"That was the Judicial police," one of us says. "They came to get their share."

Shell comes out of the office with a notebook in his hands and begins calling names until he's called twenty-five men. He tells them to get ready because they'll be leaving in the early morning hours. The news excites even those of us whose names weren't called.

THE ROBBERY

I didn't have a chance to be called because I haven't yet turned over the telephone number of my friend in Houston. I decide to get some rest. It's been two nights since I've slept well. When a bench that rests against the wall of the patio is vacated, I take the opportunity. I put my small bag and my jacket beneath my head, as pillows. But that little measure of comfort costs me dearly. Two hours later, when I wake up, both the jacket and bag have vanished. When I'm aware that they're gone, I leap to my feet like a spring, looking this way and that, and staring at everybody who's near. I ask if anybody has seen my things, but nobody knows anything. I put my hand in my pocket and am relieved to see that my billfold is still there. But the $550 to pay for the trip was sewn into the lining of the jacket. I keep asking if anyone saw anything, but the effort is useless.

Now I repent removing the jacket from my shoulders, despite the heat of Nuevo Laredo, and the grime that its fabric had accumulated. I'd had the idea that a thief would try to take my billfold, not my clothing. Deeply depressed, I walk around the place, looking everywhere in the hopes of seeing some sign of it. My only consolation is that the son-of-a-street-dog who took the jacket may not notice that it is lined with sweat, congealed in the form of green bills.

In desperation, I go to Juan Serna. He receives me in his office after I've waited half an hour outside while he talked on the telephone. I tell him about the robbery.

"Look for it," he says. "Somebody around here ought to have it."

I look closely at the others and for the first time, notice that despite the heat, many of them are wearing two layers of clothing.

About two o'clock in the morning, the names on the list are read again. Sixteen men are laid down like sardines in the floor of the station wagon. Another nine are stuffed into the blue car that had been on blocks the day before. In a matter of minutes, the

29

group is gone.

The robbery deprives me of sleep. After a long night of depression, I watch the sunrise. It's clear to me that I now have no choice except to call my friend and tell him what happened. Even though I'm worried about being robbed of the $100 I still have in my billfold, I head downtown and arrive without incident in about thirty minutes. From a booth at a public telephone, I call my friend, collect. My carelessness distresses him, but he sees that there's nothing that we can do now. We decide that I shouldn't return home; we'll just have to find a way to replace the money I've lost.

Feeling a little better, I go to a restaurant for breakfast; the scarce rations at Juan Serna's have kept me in constant hunger. I also find a public shower. About noon, I return to the house and an hour later they give us a meal of macaroni, beans and tortillas. I give Serna my friend's telephone number and he immediately orders that my name be put on a list.

That night the sky covers with clouds, and thinking that it might rain, five of us get into one of the cars under repair. But about ten o'clock, we hear the cry, "Lunch!" We all run to eat, and on returning, find that our places in the car have been occupied.

"Ah, so what?" one of us says with a mouth full of laughter. "Its just like the old saying, '*Quien va a la villa pierde su silla*'— 'He who goes to town loses his seat.' I guess we'd rather eat well than sleep well." And without ceasing to laugh, he looks at the sky, which is growing increasingly cloudy.

Having no shelter, we stretch a cloth over the concrete slab on which one the cars sits; we also hang up above us an old sheet that someone pulled from one of the vehicles. Not long afterwards, the rain begins to fall, scattered drops at first, then torrents.

We stand up in the rain, and each one of us looks for a new place to rest. The men who'd been sleeping on the patio scatter like cigarettes, crowding under the tin roof that covers the basin where the women wash clothes. I find the back seat of a car and pull it beneath one of the vehicles. Even though raindrops spatter from the sides, I'm able to sleep a few hours.

By sunrise, most of the twenty-five men who had left during the night have returned. The runners have brought in others, and altogether, some sixty "goats" are now at Juan Serna's house.

In a few minutes, we again hear Shell reading the list, this time for those who are going to Houston. I'm named along with the others. First, the car carrying nine men leaves, and then the station wagon, with sixteen more, just as before. About half an hour later, the station wagon in which I'm riding stops in front of a house. We're told to run inside. I hear the faint rumble of running water. We're on the bank of the Rio Grande.

THE RIO GRANDE

The house in which we take refuge is built in the rear of a house of concrete. It has four rooms, but in the two of them, part of the brick walls have fallen down. The roof is of asphalt sheeting. There's a badly rusted bed in each of the two better rooms. Their mattresses are filthy and stained and their coverings are torn, letting the stuffing fall out. Two cardboard boxes are stacked atop one another in one room, to make an altar, covered with a flowered print of oilcloth. On both ends of the altar are plastic drinking glasses filled with artificial flowers. A half-burned candle in the center of the altar gives a faint light to two images of the Virgin whose rusty tin frames are nailed to the wall above. At the foot of the altar, five newborn puppies are playing atop some old clothing. Upon the only plastered wall, a poorly skilled artist has painted the Virgin of Guadalupe in sad and cheap colors.

Once the twenty four of us have spread ourselves into the rooms, we wait for about an hour until a fat man arrives. He's shirtless and one of his arms bears a tattoo of an Indian maid. He says that we should be alert to a signal from the River.

Five minutes later, we hear a long and shrill whistle and the same fat man appears from behind a bush, extending five fingers as a signal that five of us should come. Ten minutes later he leans out of the bush again and makes the same signal. This goes on until only four of us are left in the hideaway shack. At the signal, we run towards the River. When we get to where the fat man is, he tells us to remove our shoes.

"The River is swollen!" one of us says when we've gotten nearer to its bank. "Two nights ago we crossed it by walking, but that's not possible now. Last night's rain made it swell."

The River *is* swollen and its swift current makes a sound like that of a coming storm. The water is dirty and thick and stained gray, like the color of the dirt on the riverbank. Pieces of wood and branches float on its surface.

A man who's standing waist-high in water near the riverbank

tells us to climb into the inflatable raft that he's holding with a rope. We squat aboard, one after another. Then the fat man swims into the water and with his free hand pulls the raft into the current.

"Don't move, you *cabrones*!" the fat man says when one of us tries to make himself comfortable.

The fat man is touching bottom when we begin, but the center of the river must be deep, because he then swims a while, and touches bottom, walking again, as we near the opposite bank. Despite his efforts, in crossing we've drifted a good ways downstream.

When we get to the American bank, we put our shoes on and reunite with the others who are hiding in a high cane break. A little later, a young, thin man tells us in a low voice that we should follow him, walking in a crouched position. For fifteen minutes we climb up and down little hills. Sometimes he tells us to wait while he advances to reconnoiter, and sometimes we run, as he tells us to, until we come to a place where houses begin. A dark man with short, curly hair is waiting for us.

"Three at a time! Run straight ahead! Further on another guy will tell you what to do," he orders.

A hundred yards further, somebody else tells us to go through a black door into a house.

From Houston to San Antonio

TEXAS

The house is of wood, with peeling paint, and it occupies about half a lot, 15 by 30 yards in size. Part of the yard is covered by grass and some struggling, potted plants. The rest is covered with asphalt.

We spread out in two big, clean rooms and, as we are told, stay silent, waiting for the others to come. By nightfall, all two dozen of us are in the house.

On this American side of the River our living conditions are better. We have a roof over our heads, a bathroom with a shower, sink and commode.

"Well, just look at this!," says a young man, leaning towards us with both hands on the door frame. He looks us over and gives us a cordial smile.

"The race tired you out, did it?" he says to one of us who is red-faced and bathed in sweat from the heat of the run.

"If you will," he says to us all, "for the sake of our security, please remain orderly and quiet."

He's the owner of the house, and he's known as Chuco. He's got an athletic complexion, and he's dressed in khaki pants with a shirt of big checks in different tones of brown. He's beltless, his short black hair is combed towards the back of his head, and his shoes are of patent leather. It's the *pachuco* style of my father's youth, or as I'd later learn in several cities, the style of today's Low Riders.

Chuco is Juan Serna's key man on the north side of the River. One of us, a man over forty who has been making trips along our route for fifteen years, says that Chuco is competent and experienced, and that his professionalism is due to having inherited the job from his father, who provided the same services for more than twenty years. He also says that Chuco has tempered over the years, and that more than once he's had to spend time in jail. Not many years ago, the man tells us, Chuco regained his liberty on bond, after having served part of a three year sentence.

"Hey, you've got no reason to go out towards the street, and much less to leave the house, okay?" Chuco says. "If you want soft drinks, cigarettes or anything else, just let us know and we'll go get them."

A deck of cards appears and somebody sets up a checkers game on a sheet of cardboard, using bottle caps for playing pieces.

Early the next morning, Chuco's young assistants get busy. They come in and go out a couple of times during the morning and later show up as drivers of a couple of cars that they park outside. One of the cars is a two-door, the other a four-door. After a while, another assistant, notebook in hand, calls several names, and without waiting for the persons named to respond, gives instructions: "Get ready to leave! Go to the bathroom if you've got to, because we're not stopping until we get to Houston."

A lot of us weren't called.

About eleven o'clock in the morning, Chuco and his assistants show nervousness. The drivers, seated on a couch in the living room, keep looking at their watches. Chuco sits in a wooden chair by the telephone, waiting.

"What could be happening to him, uh? He should have called by now," Chuco says after glancing at his watch.

The most experienced one of us lays my doubts aside. "They're waiting for their lookout to tell them when the road is clear," he explains.

The telephone rings. Chuco picks up the receiver before the first ring has stopped. He identifies himself and hangs up. He looks towards his assistants who seem nervous. One of them plays with the strings of his tennis shoes, tying and untying them. Another, sunk down in the couch, changes position every few seconds, making its springs squeak. Chuco moves his head to one side, as if saying, "Let's go!"

The guy who called the names from the list rises and holds the door open. The wets who were named crowd up around the door, each one trying to be first to get through. In a few seconds, the first car is filled and gone.

In a little while the second is filled, but Chuco says that it shouldn't leave yet.

"It's not smart for one to go very close to the other, okay? If you keep your distance, if one car is caught, the other still has a chance to get through."

Chuco gives an affectionate slap on the shoulder to the driver who, it seems, is making his first trip.

"Take it easy, man. You've got to drive like you were taking your girlfriend out, okay? Carefully, not fast or slow, just like the law says, okay? Easy, like you weren't carrying anybody but yourself. If *La Migra* gets you, you'll be in jail fifteen days, if we don't bond you out first. And you guys," Chuco says, addressing himself to the wets, "if *La Migra* catches you, don't go accusing me. You guys should get together on your story, which should be that you pooled your money to buy the car."

Everybody promised to do that.

Among those of us who are left behind is a man from the coast of Guerrero. He has dark skin and curly hair, he's short and middle aged, and he appears to be in a state between depression and exhaustion. He lies down on one of the beds and talks about his family and his dream of being able to build them a house. Another is Francisco, a vegetable peddler who hopes to increase his capital by working in the United States. He decides to take a bath. Pedro, an Indian bricklayer from Morelos, takes the other available bed. Antonio, a young farmworker, sits down on the couch and from his back pocket takes out a well-thumbed western magazine, whose pages he turns without showing much interest. There being nothing else to do, I ask an energetic young Mexican-American woman, who is part of Chuco's family, for a bar of soap to wash the thick and sticky grime from my shirt.

Chuco comes in after a while.

"Ah, so you guys got left behind this time," he says in high spirits. "Don't worry, in a while you'll leave."

Then he mentions my name and asks which of us I am.

Juan Serna hadn't called my friend. I go with Chuco to the living room and he sits on a weak chair that squeaks beneath his weight. He dials the number that he's copied into his notebook. When the phone is answered, he hands me the mouthpiece. After a short greeting, I tell my friend that I'm on the north side of the River.

"They want to know if you'll pay for me," I say, handing the mouthpiece to Chuco. I'm able to hear my friend asking when we'll arrive in Houston.

"God only knows," Chuco tells him.

During the next five days, while we wait, twenty-three other wets arrive. Five of them are from El Salvador: three women— one a college student, one a housewife and one a workingwoman— and two male farmworkers. Two Argentines with an aristocratic bearing and sixteen Mexicans are in the group, including a thirty-six-year-old preacher with a serene personality and kind eyes.

Almost every afternoon or evening, Chuco or his wife warns

us to be quiet because *La Migra* is passing nearby. Sometimes
the immigration agents park their vehicles almost in front of the
house, and leave carrying rifles on their rounds at the riverbank.

The preacher says that he's a welder by trade, but unfortunately,
a welder without equipment. He's come to the United States to
earn enough money to buy tools for a small shop that he's established in his village. He owns a few hand tools, but no machine
tools, and even though he has an electric welder, he needs an oxy-
acetylene rig. He's come several times to the United States, but
had to cut short his last trip because of a family emergency.

One afternoon, Chuco tells us that an unidentified drowned
man has been found at the river, dressed only in underwear.

In the midst of the silence that follows, the preacher says a
prayer for the poor wetback who drowned.

"Poor fellow," the preacher says with heaviness, "it's certain
that he was a wet just like us. Only God knows where he came
from and who he left waiting. Let's pray in his name because that
poor man could have been any one of us."

The preacher kneels and bows his head and claps his hands
in front of his chest. Then we hear a clean and lamentful voice.
Some of us are seated, others, standing, and on every side, strings
of smoke rise from the hands of those who were smoking cigarettes.
Some people play with their hands and others silently tap the floor
with their feet. Finally, we hear, "Amen."

After that the drivers arrive, those who days earlier had carried
the first load of us. They seem haughty and high-spirited, especially
the one who had made his maiden trip.

"Those others, they're happily in Houston," the novice says to
Juan, who has asked about our companions.

The two drivers stand in front of Chuco, telling him about
the vicissitudes of their trips, and making gestures. They adopt
looks of surprise, then of fear, and then pretend that they're at the
steering wheel, dealing with some difficulty on the road. Laughs
and gestures are intertwined. Sitting on the couch with his hands
crossed behind his head, Chuco listens with interest. The novice
asks Chuco to lend him his cassette player, then takes a cassette still
wrapped in cellophane from his pants pocket. The cassette is of
the Tigres del Norte, singing *corridos*, or ballads, about smugglers.
The novice puts the tape player to his ears, then pulls a ten-dollar
bill from his pocket and orders one of his companions to go buy a
six-pack of beer.

Already a little tipsy, the novice tells us that he earned $300 for
the trip and we also learn from him that of the total of $450 each

of us will pay, a third is for Chuco, a third for Juan Serna, and a third for the Mexican police. The drivers earn their pay from Chuco's cut.

The Salvadoran college student, a short young woman of 18, seems to always be depressed. When her depression is deepest, she sits by herself in a corner, in view of all of us. Her countrymen speak short phrases in a low voice to her, and pat her on the shoulder, trying to console her. The men in our group also speak to her, asking if she's depressed because she's left El Salvador or because she's in a hurry to get to her destination, New York. She replies by shaking her head negatively, without saying a word. Once, when her spirits are especially low, the preacher goes up to her. She is sitting on the edge of the bed, bent over her legs so that her straight, black hair hides her face from view, and she is weeping so hard that she convulses. The preacher speaks to her paternally and for a long time. A little later she comes out of the bedroom with the preacher, her head bowed a little. With her fingers, she wipes the tears from her cheeks. The preacher keeps talking to her until she smiles shyly.

It turns out that she and her companions had left San Salvador with a *coyote*, or smuggler, who brought them illegally through Mexico without incident. At the end of each day the *coyote* assigned hotel rooms to members of the group, and despite her protests, he always gave the college girl a separate room, he said, for security reasons. Before the journey was over, he told her that if she didn't cooperate, he'd abandon her on the road, and then he raped her.

Among us is also a man who calls himself a poet. He says that he's never made any money, even though some musical groups have recorded his poems as songs. He's a short, middle-aged and frail man.

Chuco learns that there's a poet among us.

"Write me a *corrido*, Mr. Poet!" he says. "I'm going to drive the car on the next trip and you'll ride at my side, okay?."

The poet promises to write the *corrido* as soon as they get to Houston.

"*Carajo*, the way things are!" Chuco says. "Everybody comes to my house, and now there's a poet."

Chuco tells us that a couple of months earlier a pair of guys came as simple wetbacks, but in the days they waited, he noticed that they behaved suspiciously. He questioned them in private, but they told him that nothing was underfoot. But some of his people searched their belongings and found packets of cocaine in their clothing.

"Some guys want to pass on the sly," he tells us, "and then, if we get caught, we've got to pay for their crimes. Haven't I got enough problems already?"

LA MIGRA

On the fifth day they make preparations for the trip. Because the preacher, Juan and I are the shortest, they put us in the trunk of the car: the preacher, Juan and me. Six more go in the seats. As soon as the driver has us loaded, he takes off.

We turn several corners on the streets of town. Then we feel the car pick up speed and that makes us think that we're on a freeway. I am on one side of the trunk, the preacher is in the middle, and Juan is on the other side. The floor of the trunk is lacking the carpet that it probably once had, and it's not very comfortable riding upon a sheet of pressed steel. Just above my head are vents that allow me to see the clear sky. It is deep blue. The vents were apparently created, or left in the car when its rear sound speakers were removed. At least, through them I'm able to breathe air that isn't as hot as the air from the trunk. Besides giving me air and a view of the sky, the vents let me see up into the rear windshield, which is big enough and curved enough to work as a kind of periscope. I can see reflections in it of the four guys in the back seat, and of the two who are riding next to the driver who is smoking. I can even glimpse at the road ahead.

"I hope we arrive," Juan says.

"God willing," the preacher responds.

I tell them about the panorama I can see, but they don't take heart. "From here I can see when the *Migra* shows," I tell them, to ease the tension that has overtaken us.

They don't take kindly to my remark. "Shut up, man. Don't even think about that," the preacher says.

After about half an hour, the trunk is uncomfortably hot. Because I'm close to the tire, it's completely impossible for me to stay still. The sheet steel beneath me little by little grows hotter until I have to change positions. I feel like a roasting chicken and I don't want to imagine how much hotter it could become. I inform the other two and Juan hands me his jacket. I wad it up and put it between my back and the steel and it gives me some relief.

We make some quick comments about those who are riding in the seats, and conclude that they aren't as comfortable as might seem.

"Right now," Juan says, "some of them probably have numb legs."

"Accidents happen all the time," the preacher says, "and we're neither the first nor the last to travel in a trunk."

Such comments are nothing more than a manner of infusing ourselves with confidence, because anecdotes always come to mind. In the house of Juan Serna, a wet told us that he'd seen three others fried like bacon in a trunk. The tragedy happened when the car in which they were riding caught fire. The driver, foreseeing that the police would come, took flight and perhaps without thinking, took the keys with him. There was no way to get the men out who were in the trunk. I look at the preacher to see what spirits he's in, and I see that his eyes are closed and his lips are moving rapidly, as if he's in prayer.

The car makes some turns. We leave the pavement, go onto a dirt road, and just as quickly return to pavement again. We know this because on pavement the rattling stops and on dirt roads, the bumping and noise starts up again, throwing us about like dice in a gambler's hand. Some little holes in the floor of the trunk let dust in, and little by little, a cloud of dust forms in our space. Juan puts a handkerchief over his nose and the preacher fans the air with his hands in vain.

"All of this to get to Houston," the preacher says.

"When we get there, we're really going to need a bath," Juan comments.

From my observatory I see passing scenes of land covered with dry, yellow grass, and every few seconds, lines of barbed wire pass before my view. Sometimes I see a thing or two that's further off.

About two hours later, the driver utters a profanity that Jesus himself may have heard, and that probably offended the Virgin. With the fist of his right hand he beats upon the steering wheel. He brakes sharply, shaking us, and the tires of the car skid in the dirt. "Run!" we hear him shout, and immediately we hear the doors opening. Those of us in the trunk know that the trip has been frustrated, but we don't want to believe it.

The sound of a car comes closer and it brakes next to us. I can see it clearly in the reflections of the windshield. It's a light green car, a *Migra* patrol car, but I don't tell my companions this because they will see it soon enough, and I don't want to be the bird who brings bad news.

We hear the sound of the car's door opening and closing.

"Why are you running, you idiot!" we hear somebody shout in badly pronounced Spanish. Inside the car, only one of our companions is left.

We hear slow and heavy steps close to our car, then the sound of a key being placed in the lock. Above us, a blond Anglo holds open the door of the trunk. He's tall and bald, and wearing a dark green uniform. A pipe rests between his lips.

He smiles in a joking and friendly way.

"How comfortable you are," he says wryly. "Get out."

When the three of us are outside, he tells us to sit on the tail of the car without closing the trunk. The rest of our companions are lined up against the side of the car with the exception of one, who is climbing a barbed wire fence, on his way back. He must have been the one to whom the word "idiot" was addressed. Looking at the terrain behind us, it's clear that escape is impossible. The land is a plain of dried grass and its few bushes don't even have leaves. Us captives lament what's happened by exchanging glances and making gestures with our heads. But then I notice that the driver is missing.

The agent comes and goes in front of us, unhurried and unworried. He takes long, heavy steps and looks us over closely, as if we were exhibiting ourselves.

"Which one of you is the driver?" he suddenly asks.

"None of us," three voices answer.

The agent goes over to his car, takes out a walkie-talkie, speaks with someone, and then comes back. He is smiling triumphantly.

"Where did you think you were going?" he asks.

"To Houston," one of us says.

Then he asks how much we were to pay. "Why did you decide to come now?" he says, enjoying himself. "Why couldn't you wait until tomorrow? That's my day off!"

"Let us go," Juan says.

The agent laughs.

"No, that's not possible," he says, still in high spirits. "You guys ought to go back to Mexico and find a smarter coyote."

"Are all of you Mexicans?" he asked, scrutinizing us. "You're Salvadoran," he suddenly says, pointing to the preacher.

"I am Mexican," the preacher serenely answers. "I'm more Mexican than Emiliano Zapata."

After a long silence the agent says, "If you are carrying a pistol, knife, cocaine or marijuana, take it out and hand it over."

Nobody answers.

"At last," the agent says, perhaps just to break the silence, "are you going to tell me who the driver is?"

A few minutes later two Border Patrol vehicles pull up. One is like the car that showed up first, the other is a van, one of those that we wetbacks know as "*perreras*," or dog wagons.

The agent who stopped us points in the direction in which the driver escaped. His companions make use of their radios. They order us to get into the *perrera* where we encounter eight other wets. The windows of the *perrera* are covered with heavy metal screens.

A half hour later, we find ourselves in the Immigration offices in the little south Texas town of Hebbronville; they consist of three, one-story buildings arranged in the form of a U on one side of a highway. The middle of the U is a paved parking lot where three more patrol vehicles are stationed. Nine of us are locked in a cell in one of the buildings. Inside the building are ten agents, most of them Mexican-Americans, who go back and forth from outside into the office. A couple of them sit in chairs behind desks.

A bronze-skinned agent with a sparse moustache comes up to our cell and recites the following words: "You are detained for having illegally entered the country. We are going to investigate you, but first you must know your rights. You can refuse to answer our questions and you can request the presence of an attorney, and if you don't have one, we'll provide one."

None of us asks for an attorney.

Our cell has three concrete walls, and the side that looks out onto the office is covered by a wire screen. Inside the cell are urinals, a sink and concrete benches. A few minutes pass before they call us, one by one, to make our statements.

The questions: How many times have you been detained by Immigration agents? Have you ever been arrested by the police? Where were you born? What are the names of your parents? Where do you come from?

The agent who questions me also writes down my physical description. He hands me the form with my answers written upon it, gives me a pen, and points to the spot where I should sign, beneath a paragraph saying that I voluntarily leave the country for having infringed upon its laws.

When I walk back towards the cell, I discover that they've also detained the driver. He's short and skinny. His slightly oval face is stained by sweat that has dried, and grains of sand seem to have impregnated his pores. They have him handcuffed in a cell two doors down from us. He's seated in a chair and his slumped body gives the impression that at any minute, he might fall down. His eyes are deeply sad, melancholy. His condition makes me feel sorry for him. He is the image of a condemned man.

Upon seeing me his eyes dart left and right, and seeing that none of the agents is looking, to my surprise he lets his face adopt a look of absolute tranquility, as if in possession of himself. He makes a sign, raising his right index finger to his lips, even though to do it he has to move both hands because he's cuffed. He tells me not to say anything about him. I move my head a little to show him that they haven't asked me about him. He seems convinced. To my admiration, he then returns to looking sad. He should have been an actor in the theatre.

When they've interrogated all of us, they call us in alphabetical order towards the door where an agent hands us a copy of the paper we've signed. Another agent is waiting for us at the door of the *perrera*.

"And this?" Juan asks when they hand him his paper. "Is this our passport?"

"Yeah, sure it is. It's the passport to your country," an agent says, savoring Juan's quip.

In less than half an hour they discharge us at the entrance to the international bridge in Laredo. Each one of us pays ten American cents and we walk in silence over the bridge.

Meanwhile, I try to gather my thoughts, to decide if I should cross again or not. I've run into complications now for more than two weeks, and I can't image that a new attempt would be any easier. The possibility of returning home turns around in my head, but I also think that I already owe a sum of dollars, and I'm now at the border.

"What are you going to do, Juan?," I ask, because he's the most experienced among us.

He turns toward me, looking at my shoulders with his tired eyes and with an air of certainty he says, "Well, what else? Cross again!"

TO HOUSTON

As soon as we're in Nuevo Laredo I go to a phone booth where long distance calls can be made. I talk to my friend and tell him that *La Migra* has spoiled our attempt. The most logical thing is for me to go back to Juan Serna's house and wait for a second chance, but my friend tells me to let him think about other possibilities, and to call him again later in the day. He says something about helping me cross on a road that he knows well.

While waiting for the hour to call again, I go to a restaurant downtown and take a seat to eat. As hungry as I am, I feel capable of gulping down everything on the menu. But my stomach has shrunk during these days of small rations and it no longer has the capacity that it did in my village when it could easily hold three tortillas, fresh from the *comal* and bigger than a long-play record, plus plates of food. Today I content myself with only a piece of beef steak bathed in tomato sauce and peppers, a handful of beans and a couple of little tortillas made by machine.

Later on, when I talk to my friend, he tells me that he's decided to come for me himself, and that in order to do it, he's gotten permission to take time off from his job. According to his instructions, I have to go to a different bordertown. I arrive the next day, several hours before my friend is due. The town is quieter than Nuevo Laredo. Almost all commerce is confined in stores; there are almost no portable stalls or peddlers here, just a few vendors on three-wheeled, bicycle-like vehicles.

My friend is legally in the U.S. He comes across the border to meet me. When he arrives, we walk toward the edge of town until we come to a neighborhood of dirt streets and unplastered houses. The older houses have walls of adobe and roofs of Spanish tile, and the newer ones, walls of concrete block and roofs of tin sheeting. In a lot of them, windows are covered with strips of vinyl or with sheets of cardboard, and their badly mounted doors are made of old wood.

My friend says that the neighborhood hasn't changed in years

48

and that it'll be easy to find the house he's looking for. It's a place with walls of cement block and a roof of asphalt sheeting, with a dirt floor and a kerosene stove. We are met by a tall, thin, near-sighted woman who wears thick eyeglasses, and four little children who are playing with plastic cars on the ground. The house is small. While we wait for her husband to come, the woman invites us to sit down on some metal chairs whose backrests are marked with the logo of a beer company. After a while, the man my friend knows arrives. He's a man of about forty, tall and strong-looking. He and my friend greet each other affectionately and my friend explains that he needs the man to take me to the other side of the River. My friend's contact is a "*patero*" or "duck man," not a *coyote*. His job isn't to get me to Houston, it's just to get me across the River. We immediately arrange for the crossing to take place that same night, and we pay the man $20 in advance.

Before returning to the north side of the River, my friend gives me the name, telephone and room number of the motel where he's staying. I write this information on my palm while memorizing it. When nightfall comes, I present myself at the house of the duck man, who is already waiting for me. Before leaving the house with me, I see him put a black roll of rubber beneath his arm. It's the inner tube of a truck tire, and that's what we'll use as a raft in the River. We leave the house and walk a shadowy route; the streetlights don't have any bulbs. As we're leaving, we hear his wife say blessings. With the house soon behind us, we hike through the wilds surrounded by bushes that aren't ten feet tall and don't have many branches. We pass by a barn, and then come to another section of raw land. We climb over several barbed wire fences until we can clearly hear the rumble of the River's current. On a little hill above the bank, I see the Rio Grande snaking up and down its course. In some places it seems quiet and inoffensive, in others, almost invisible, but then it'll take on the look of a wide and silvery sheet of metal. But on its curves, it looks too fierce to approach.

We go upriver a couple of hundred yards until we come to a place where the channel is wide. There on the bank the duck man inflates the inner tube by blowing air into it with his mouth. The job tires him a bit, and from time to time I have to help him. With my shoes and my pants tied on my head, I follow him into the current, but before it reaches my chest, the duck man, who is dressed only in briefs, having left his clothes in the bushes, prostrates himself in the water. He begins swimming, pulling the innertube with one hand. I climb inside it. It's all as easy as when I crossed at

Nuevo Laredo. When we get to the American side I put my clothes
on and we walk among the canebreaks until we come to a dirt road
where the duck man leans out, then makes hand signs that tell me
to follow him. We run across the dirt road and stop about a hundred yards beyond. From there the duck man points me towards
a blue light which he says I should use as my guide because the
place my friend is waiting is located to one side of it. Before saying so-long, the duck man tells me to be careful, and to look in
every direction before advancing. Then he says that he hopes God
will accompany me on the rest of my road.

I want to get this over with, and I take off running through the
brush as fast as my legs will carry me. There's a bright light shining in the distance, and it illuminates almost everything around,
there being no hills. I run in a crouched position for fear that
the light will give me away. In my hurry I run squarely into a
growth of cactus. Its spines stick in my thighs and arms. With my
body heated by the exercise I'm getting, the pain isn't nearly as
persuasive as my nervousness to arrive, but after a while I feel myself pricked at every step and I have to stop to remove the cactus
spines. Then I begin to sweat in a great stream. I have to breathe
through my mouth because my nose isn't enough and my legs feel
tired because at almost every step I'm breaching a path through the
weeds. Though I feel tired, I don't think of sitting down to rest.
Before my eyes, getting closer all the time, is a freeway where I see
the conical, fleeting lights of cars that come and go and disappear
in the distance.

When I'm about thirty yards away, I see a red and blue light on
the roof of a car parked at the side of the freeway, almost exactly
where I calculate that I'll have to cross. I stop and sit down behind
a *huizache* plant. The car I see could be the Border Patrol or the
police and it could also be nothing, but I'm going to wait until
it moves. It does leave, but only after several minutes, enough
time for my sweat to dry and my tiredness to disappear. My only
discomforts are thirst and dried lips. I run up to the edge of the
freeway and then, in a moment when there's no traffic, cross at a
leisurely walk, in case the *Migra* is spying from some dark corner.
As calmly as in the streets of my village, I walk to the hotel and
start looking for my friend's room number.

When I find him he tells me to wait in the room while he goes to
take a drive. He says he'll be back in half an hour and tells me not
to answer the door, if anyone knocks, and to ignore the telephone
if it rings. In less than half an hour he returns only to tell me
to get into the car. Then he drives onto the freeway. My friend is

nervous. He says that we've got to get to a certain place before we'll be out of danger, and mentions a town with a name in English. He also tells me that if *La Migra* stops us, I should say that he picked me up at the side of the road. Given my tired appearance, that story wouldn't be hard to sell. My friend smokes one cigarette after another and almost measures the mileage himself, telling me every few minutes how much distance is left between us and the town he mentioned.

I'm still thirsty and I tell him so. He remembers that he bought a six-pack of soft drinks and that it is sitting on the back seat. I find the package and, in long and desperate swigs, I drink the contents of two cans. Once my thirst is quenched, I roll down the window and throw the cans out.

"Never do that again!" my friend tells me, more surprised than irritated. "That's a crime in the United States! We're still in a danger zone and just for throwing out trash the police could stop us. You'd be crossing the River again before long, but I'd be in jail."

I say I'm sorry, that it was only ignorance of the laws that made me do that, and that fortunately, neither the police nor *La Migra* were in sight.

The lights of the car illuminate a perfectly maintained road. We've gone several miles, no potholes have shaken our seats, and my friend hasn't had to detour his course to avoid them, either. When we reach a point where my friend tells me that we're out of danger, he relaxes a little. We stop to pick up a couple of sandwiches of barbecued beef, Texas style, along with french fries. We eat on the road. The comfort of the trip makes sleep overtake me. I spend so long sleeping that the trip to Houston seems short to me. After we've turned a few corners in the city, the experience of the border seems far away.

If, in this account, I haven't given specific information about my friend, nor the place where I crossed the River with his help, it may be because I'll need them again, and I don't want to make a sure route known to *La Migra*. For me, it represents a savings of several hundred dollars and a lot of time spent waiting for *coyotes* and, above all, freedom from the fear of riding in a trunk again. On the trip my friend and I made, there were only the two of us and I had a seat to myself.

THE MAGNOLIA DISTRICT

The next day in Houston, my friend lends me more money, enough to rent an apartment in the Magnolia district, not far from the Houston ship channel. For sixty dollars a week I occupy a room on a piece of property that is about twenty feet wide by sixty feet long, enclosed by a chain link fence, except on the side that faces the street. One of the rooms, the one that faces the street, is made of wood, with a triangle-shaped roof and shingles of green, almost the same shade as its green walls. It appears to be the oldest, the best-constructed, but also the most deteriorated room, probably having been at one time the only building on the lot. The other rooms are located in what was probably once a garden or yard. The passageway through which I must walk to reach my room probably once led to a driveway. This seems to be true because the rooms located in other than the principal house seem to have been provisionally built, without any design. They're just wooden cubes with slightly inclined roofs of aluminum sheeting. Each one has a single door and a window that is covered with fine screen.

The room I occupy is at the foot of the property, and in earlier times it looked a lot like the principal house, probably having been the garage, now converted to living space. Mine is a one-story place with a shower and both hot and cold water. I've got a four-burner stove and a refrigerator. My cooking utensils consist of a frying pan and a spoon, and that's enough for me. The wooden floor is covered with linoleum in a red tile pattern, and the walls, with a plastic material printed to imitate the look of pinewood paneling. There are two windows in my room, but the glass in one of them has disappeared, and in its placed someone has placed a sheet of thin plastic, affixed with masking tape. Through its gaps I can feel the cold winter air. The place is unfurnished, but fortunately, I've found an old mattress that I spread out on the floor, covering myself with sheets my friend loaned me.

The owner of the apartments is a Mexican who's been a legal resident of the United States for many years. He's about fifty, short

of stature, with a light complexion and a round face. His name is
Anselmo Mendoza, and he told me that he'll come around every
Sunday to collect the rent.

The neighborhood is distinctively Hispanic. I don't see a single
gringo in the streets, which are paved and well-laid out, but full
of potholes. The flower beds between the sidewalks and street are
poorly kept, some of them being overgrown, others bald. Most
of the houses in the area are of wood, although some have been
covered with aluminum siding. Almost all are surrounded by chain
link fences, from whose posts clotheslines hang. Very few have
well-kept gardens with grass, flowers, bushes and walkways, and
some peoples' yards are covered with gravel. Everywhere in the
yards children are riding tricycles or big plastic cars that they move
with their feet.

On the other side of the house fences, dogs greet me with fierce
barking as soon as I come close to the property lines. They follow
my steps as if they were ready to tear my feet to shreds with their
teeth, if it weren't for the fence between us, and I still hear them
barking even after I've put a good deal of distance between me and
their turf. All of the houses have screened doors and windows, and
some of the screens are the color of rust. Others are new, to judge
by their leaden color. In some places, I can't distinguish these
houses from those on the Mexican border; the neglect of paint
has left them almost bare, and in their yards, weeds and flowering
plants have grown together in confusion. There are also beer joints
on every side, many of them constructed in former garages of sheet
metal, each with signs saying "Lounge" after a name in Spanish.

About four blocks away are *taquerías*, miscellany, ice cream
shops, hamburger joints, and bakeries. Some of the stores have
signs advertising Mexican products like *Mejoral*. But they're all
too small to imagine finding work in them. I also see the residues
of the petroleum boom of the early '80's. At almost every corner I encounter railroad lines, or yards where pipe and other oilfield equipment is stored. There are small factories that have signs
saying that they make oilfield valves, and workshops that repair
diesel and electric motors. But they're all either small operations,
or they're closed, or someone has already told me that they've got
no openings. I've also asked at a warehouse containing—I didn't
know what. I saw trucks coming and going, but when I asked about
jobs, I was told that no hiring was being done.

A SOCIAL SECURITY CARD

The people I encounter in the streets are all Hispanics, but meeting them doesn't give me much pleasure because a lot of them, like me, are walking around looking for work. Some have asked me where they might find a job. I take this to mean that unemployment is high, and that those people who've just arrived, like me, only add to the problem. One person who helps me is a guy who runs a taco stand. He tells me that to get work I'll need a Social Security card and number—something I'd surmised from talking to my friend—and that fake cards are available. The guy at the taco stand says that employers never pay attention to the cards themselves, just to the numbers. He also tells me where I could buy one.

He tells me that the good times are past in Houston. There was a time, he says, during which contractors went looking for workers in the streets. So many people came to town that shelter was in short supply. The landlords had to divide bedrooms in their apartments, and even people who weren't landlords cleared spaces in their homes, threw out mattresses, and took in renters. But now many houses are vacant, and though the demand for workers has fallen, wetbacks keep coming, especially from Central America.

"But don't give up," the taco vendor tells me. "The prospects are not very bright, but the city continues living. There are people, and businesses, not like in the years past, but we are still here, and we're still surviving. If you have patience, sooner or later you will find work," he urges me.

Without giving it much more thought, after speaking to him I go to hunt the place where I can buy a Social Security card. It's a used car lot, located on a corner. About fifteen cars are parked there, each one with a price painted in big white characters on its front windshield. One of the cars has its hood raised, and beneath it a guy in greasy overalls is working on a motor. His body is doubled over, half-in, half-out.

I say hello and tell him I need a Social Security card. He raises

his head. His black hair falls to his shoulders. He looks at me for
an instant, returns to his work, and asks in a Mexican- American
accent if I have brought the Social Security number with me.

"I didn't bring it," I reply.

"Ah," he says, "you want me to invent it for you, isn't that it?"
I don't answer, because I don't know if I can trust him.

"Wait a minute," he says after a little hesitation. "I'm about to
finish this piddling job."

Half an hour later he shows me into his little office. Among
tools and motor parts and dirty rags is a formica-topped desk on
which a big typewriter and a little television sit. In order to sit
down, he's got to put aside a box containing bolts and screws that
was upon his chair. Then he takes a card out of a box in his desk,
puts it in the typewriter, and asks me my name. He writes it down
and after looking at the metal roof while thinking, he hurriedly
types nine numbers on the card, which has blue printing on both
sides. He tells me that I owe him five dollars. I pay him, say thanks
and go away satisfied with my false acquisition.

Once I'm in the street I turn the card over in my hand several
times, wondering what its words say. At one of the many shops in
the neighborhood that sell magazines in Spanish, I buy an English-
Spanish dictionary. Later I spend more than an hour at a table in
a hamburger joint, looking up the meanings, word by word. When
I've deciphered them, I'm not as proud as I was at first. What I
wanted was a card to use for fooling employers, but this one may
not work. On its face the card shows two pillars, one at each extreme, united by a line in the form of an arch, exactly like the
legitimate cards I'll see later. On the arched lines are the words
SOCIAL SECURITY, in the same style as on genuine cards, but
beneath the arch, in smaller letters, are the words, "Not Issued by
the United States Government." On the opposite side are three
clarifications, one of which says, "No intent exists to harm or de-
fraud any city, company or person." Who can such a card fool?
Probably, only someone like me. Surely there will be other wets
who'll also pay five dollars to be fooled. But still, I do not throw
the card away as I ought to. I put it in my billfold, where I've kept
a few reminders of Mexico, including a 1000-peso bill.

ENGLISH PHRASES

Several days have passed without any results. Disillusioned, I see that nothing is as simple as I imagined before coming to the United States. Before leaving home, I thought the trip would be simple. Arrive, go to work, receive dollars immediately, and someday go back like my townsmen, if not driving a luxurious car, with at least something to show for my efforts. I ask myself if they, too, passed through the same difficulties that I'm encountering in Houston. For moments I am assaulted by the idea that it would be more intelligent to go back home to the carpentry workshop, because there was no shortage of work there, even if the money I made wasn't much. But every time this idea runs around my head, I squash it like you would a cockroach, like something undesirable. I don't have any right to resolve my problems by going back. I owe a debt to my friend and I can't return home with nothing in my pockets.

So I keep walking from block to block, store to store. Whenever I encounter *gringos* in charge, I say the same thing: "Excuse me, sir, I'm looking for job." At least that's something new. In a pocket notebook I've written a bunch of phrases in English. If I go into a restaurant, to my usual phrase I add, "like dishwasher," and in a mechanical shop or warehouse, I add, "like helper." I have also learned how to answer in case they ask me, "Do you speak English?" I say, "No, but I'm good worker." I have the expressions written in English and the way to pronounce them written in Spanish and sometimes when I'm walking on a lonely block, I practice them aloud.

Following the advice of other wetbacks, I also stand outside big hardware and garden shops and lumberyards, in case the buyers who come for materials need helpers. I stand in the entrances, but after a few days, I see that the effort is futile. Nobody has asked for help even carrying purchases to the parking lots.

A Spanish-language newspaper circulates in the neighborhood, but it's classified ads haven't been of much use in seeking work.

It costs twenty-five cents and is similar to our provincial newspapers, because it doesn't have many pages and most of its space is devoted to photographs. In every issue, one of its pages carries a cartoon strip by a guy named Antonio Eduardo Licón. Its title is ZOPILOTE Y MR. MIGRA, or BUZZARD AND MR. MIGRA. Licón draws the wetback as shoeless and ragged, always trying various ruses to outwit Mr. Migra, a typical *gringo*-looking guy, who always foils Zopilote's attempts to get into the United States. One of the cartoons, for example, shows Zopilote amongst cattle in a truck headed for an international bridge. Zopilote has made a cow's head for himself. Mr. Migra looks into the truck from above and sees nothing unusual. But when he looks at the bottom of the bed, he notes that one of the cows doesn't have hoofs. Barefoot Zopilote gets sent back to Mexico again.

ABEL

While walking the streets I encounter a wetback named Abel who tells me that he doesn't know where to find steady work, but that every morning he goes to a radio station, KLVL, to listen to a Spanish-language program called "I Need a Job." Employers call the station, offering work. It's about three o'clock in the afternoon when he tells me this.

Abel, too, has been looking for work, but says that in the afternoons, little is to be found. He takes me to the studio, so that I'll know how to find it. It's in a one-story building with two salons under one metal roof. Only its big antennas and an almost invisible sign announce that it's KLVL.

"Tomorrow you'll have to be here before ten o'clock," Abel tells me.

"Have you found work by coming to this station?" I ask.

"Only temporary jobs, and it's been a while since I found any work of any kind. But I'm living with some guys who do have jobs and they give me a place to sleep and food. Otherwise, I'd be in the street."

"I haven't worked since coming here nearly a month ago," I tell him.

Abel is short and thin. He's wearing tennis shoes and worn-out khaki pants, a colored cotton t-shirt, a thin casual jacket, and a nylon gimme cap. He's says that he came to the United States three years earlier, when he was fourteen.

"And your parents gave you permission to leave, being so young?" I ask, thinking that my parents would never have let me leave at that age.

"They are poor, very poor," he says while pulling on the brim of his hat and looking downwards, as if recalling his parents saddened him. "I promised to help them, so they had to let me come," he adds.

The first time he came, he crossed at El Paso with only 300 pesos, but he had the good fortune to meet an older man who gave him a job on a ranch. A few months later, he joined a caravan of wets who went to California for the harvests, and ever since then, he's been on the move, working in various parts of the United States: the state of Washington, Colorado, Pennsylvania, Florida, and for a while in Chicago, St. Louis and Fort Worth. During his three years, he tells me, he's gone home only once, and at that time, he claims, he left his parents with $7,000 that he had saved.

He tells me his story with a tone of pride that makes me feel envy. To go home with that much money is what I'd like to do, and sometimes I can't sleep for thinking about it. But it seems that for me it's only a dream, and it could be only a fantasy of his, too.

"When I go back home, I want to go in a car from here," he says.

"Does that mean that you don't plan to stay in the United States?" I ask him.

"No, what are you talking about? I wouldn't want to live here!" he says making a grimace as if the United States left a bad taste in his mouth. "Here, almost everybody you see is an old drug addict or a young drug addict, and where I come from, we don't put up with that bullshit. There it's a lot if we get drunk every now and then, but nobody stays high all of the time, like some of the drug addicts I've known here in the United States."

I haven't eaten since leaving the house in the morning, and when we pass a hamburger joint, I invite Abel to join me.

"I hardly eat out," he says. "These sandwiches with meat, you should know what they make them from. My friends tell me that hamburger is made from scraps of meat. You grind it up and there you've got it. What I do is buy some eggs and a piece of sausage, and cook them in the house. That way I save money, too. A carton of eggs will last me two days, and it doesn't cost me as much as one hamburger. If you want, we can buy some things in a store and take them to my house to cook."

His idea doesn't seem so bad to me. Three years in the United States have taught him how to survive, and his ideas about savings fit my situation. My resources are shrinking every day.

Abel's place is an old wooden house with peeling white paint. Its shingled roof has been patched with sheets of metal. The window frames are rotted and their screens are rusted. Its front door is dirty from constant use, and its wood has been eaten away by changes in the position of the hasp that holds its lock. Inside, two single beds with metal frames are pushed against a wall, and a mattress is on the floor, all of them with their coverings tangled. The bathroom faucets are rusted and the mirror of the medicine cabinet is cracked down its middle. Somebody has carried off the perforated shower head, leaving only a bare pipe. The kitchen is equipped with a four-burner stove, but has no sink; they wash dishes in the bathroom. While he's frying the eggs, I ask him if the guys he is living with are family members, or if they come from his town.

"One is from Zacatecas," he says. "The other is from San Luis Potosí, and me from Chihuahua. They were already living here when I met them, four months ago, the same time that I've been without steady work. One day I met them, just like I met you, and when they found out that I didn't have any place to live, they gave me the opportunity to stay here. They're good friends."

"Have at it!" he says while putting two plates on the table. Then he divides the eggs into two parts. "Let's keep track of what we're eating. It is two chickens each, isn't it?"

"Some chickens, chicken fetuses," I say.

"Ah, it's the same. The thing is, they kill hunger," he says.

He opens one of the doors of a kitchen cabinet and takes out a couple of cans of Coke.

"In Mexico, we are poor," he says. "Here we still live like poor people, but if we can only work a little while, when we go back home with dollars we'll seem like rich men. Have you seen the houses of the rich *gringos*?"

"Only from a distance," I tell him.

"Well, I went to work in one of them with a gardener. In those houses, everything is new, everything shines, the carpet, the furniture, the walls, the decorations. In the kitchen you don't see any trash and I think they even spray perfume, because it smells that way."

"I imagine they have maids," I say.

"Sure they do, and the maids are Mexican or Central American girls," he tells me.

"Well, let's see if we have any luck at the radio station tomorrow," I say after eating.

"Yeah," he says, "let's see if we have luck. If it's not one day, it has to be the next."

Talking to Abel lifts my spirits. He and his friends are almost like the pioneer wetbacks. They came without a friend, relative or boss to receive them. They've had to establish themselves by their own efforts, alone. Abel has been in the United States for three years and still hasn't given up. From their lives I see that to make oneself comfortable here can take months or years; a lot depends upon one's tenacity and luck.

THE RADIO STATION

Early the next morning I go to the radio station, where a number of men and women—but not Abel—are already waiting to take part in the program, "I Need a Job." A few minutes later the doors of the studio open. Everybody goes in and takes a seat. There are about a dozen benches, which quickly fill. Then people come in and stand against the walls. After that, people come in and sit on the carpet in the space between the two rows of benches. The room isn't big, about 15' x 15', but about a hundred people crowd in. Among us is a woman with a baby in arms.

At ten o'clock on the dot we hear over a speaker that's mounted in one corner of the ceiling: "Friends and radio neighbors," the announcer says in Spanish, "at this time every day, Monday through Friday, we bring you the program 'I Need a Job,' with the intention of helping alleviate the serious problem of unemployment. We hope to be able to help most of the people who are today in our studio. We invite businessmen, contractors and housewives to look for employees through our program. If you need workers, all you have to do is call us. If you need work, come to our studio." Then he reads the list of jobs. "A woman is needed to do domestic work and take care of one child, salary, eighty dollars a week ... A baker with experience is needed to make Mexican breads, salary by personal arrangement ... Waitress are needed for a nightclub, salary by personal arrangement ... "

At 10:15 when the program ends the announcer says that those of us in the studio should form a line at the secretary's desk to ask for the addresses and telephone numbers of job offers that interest us. For me, there was nothing. Other people take out slips of paper or notebooks and maps of the municipal bus system, asking how to get to the places whose addresses they're given.

Others who had no luck have gathered on a corner half a block away. They lean against the wall of a place called El Charro Club, and warm themselves in the rays of the sun. I join the group of about twenty men. They greet each other with handshakes, talking like old friends. They seem unworried by the dearth of jobs.

Among them is a guy whom they call "Chesperito," who is short, chubby and about twenty-five. He's wearing two shirts and two sets of pants, and on his head there's a cap with long ears. Although he's not completely ragged, his clothing is completely dirty, and he carries with him a bundle of clothes tied with a cord, which he uses as a seat on the sidewalk. He seems to be in high spirits and he jokes with the other guys.

Also in the group is a man about sixty-five years old, who is wrapped in a black gabardine jacket, black gloves, a fedora, also black, and a gray muffler. His face is bronze and his short moustache is turning white with age. He walks erect with measured steps, and when he speaks, he adopts an air of authority, like a man who knows everything.

He says that he's retired and doesn't need to work because every week he gets a check from the government. He claims to have come to the United States long ago, as a *bracero*. He tells me that he worked in construction, in the fields, as a window- washer on skyscrapers, as a janitor, a dishwasher and many other things. He pauses when mentioning each job, as if by recalling them, he could relive again the work that he once did.

Just across from our corner is a playground for children. Its swing sets are painted in bright colors, but the place seems abandoned, perhaps because of the cold. A couple of Chicano guys are walking along the fence that surrounds it. They are wearing jeans and plaid shirts, untucked at the waist, and their hair is long and tied in turbans with red handkerchiefs, Low Rider style. The old man in black gabardine watches them until they've passed.

"How sad the youth of today is. In my time, we went to the park looking for a piece of ass," he says, making the shape of a woman with his hands. "Today it's not like that. Our kids go around looking for better pot."

Talking with the others, I learn that it's possible to find temporary jobs by standing on our corner, which for many years has been a spot where unemployed men get together every day, beginning about six in the morning. Contractors come past to hire.

But as the rest of the day goes by, no contractors show, and nobody is contracted by anybody. Meanwhile, we spend our time talking and listening to the experienced men give advice. They say that it's best to get paid in cash, every day, not by check, because some contractors have given hot checks. They also say that for a few weeks after hurricane Alicia came through Houston in 1983, clean-up jobs were plentiful.

About three o'clock the group begins breaking up little by little, everybody going in a different direction. Chesperito says that he's going to a mission where they give homeless men food and a place to sleep.

About the time I start to leave, a middle-aged man goes up to the door of the Charro Club. He opens it and behind him come two more men who go inside with him. Minutes afterwards, we hear the sound of a high-pressure hose, washing the floor, and also the noise of a broom. A tattered man comes to the door and without announcing himself, goes inside and shortly comes out carrying on his shoulders a plastic bag filled with empty beer cans. Slowly he walks away from the cantina.

THE PERUVIAN

Early the next morning, I join the group on the corner. The man in gabardine is there, Chesperito also shows up. Most of the faces I already know from the day before. The hours pass and no one is contracted. At ten o'clock, several of us go off to the radio station. There, too, I see the same faces as the day before. At the program's end I leave and go back to the corner. Today there are more people, about thirty in all. A few hours later a pickup with two Chicanos inside cruises by. The one at the steering wheel is toying with an unlit cigarette between his lips, the one on the passenger side has a sparse but long moustache.

"I need five men to do hard work," the one with the moustache says as soon as the pickup comes to a stop at the corner.

Immediately, people converge on the pickup, surrounding it completely. About fifteen guys jump onto its bed, while others, with shouts, ask those in the cabin how much the job pays, where the job site is, and what kind of work they have in mind. The Chicanos barely pay any attention. The one on the driver's side opens his door and stares at those who've jumped into the back. He studies them and points, "You ... You ... You," until he gets to five, »The rest of you, get out." One by one those who weren't chosen jump to the ground, until only the selected ones are left.

For several days I've gone to the radio station and with a few exceptions, the faces I see are those of people I saw on the first day. Every morning the woman with the child in her arms shows up, and the man in black gabardine and the black fedora is always at the corner, and so is Chesperito, whom I've never seen run towards the pickups that arrive. Abel also shows up, usually very early, and goes to the radio station, sometimes with me.

This morning on the list of jobs that the announcer reads is one saying, "House painters are needed at five dollars an hour." I'm not a painter, but it doesn't seem to me that it can be very hard to dip a brush and slap paint onto a wall. Five others think like I do, and we go up to the secretary, who gives us slips of paper that state the name, address and phone number of the contractor. One of the five of us has a car and a map of the city. He opens his map on the hood of his car, and finds the spot. He and another man are about to leave when I go up and ask for a ride. The other two do the same. The guys inside the car look at each other without saying anything.

"Five dollars a head," the one at the steering wheel says.

I'm willing to pay, but one of us, who says he's a Peruvian, tells the driver that he doesn't have any money, and asks to be taken for free, paying only if we get the promised jobs. The driver lets him in.

We drive on freeways for about half an hour, until the driver turns off on a silent street and comes to a place where a series of new apartments are under construction. The complex is so big that we can't see the end of it. While waiting for the driver to find the foreman, we see that about fifteen men are already working, each one with a brush in one hand and a gallon of paint in the other. They're painting door and window frames.

The contractor is an Anglo who doesn't say a word to us while sitting inside his van. He sounds the horn for a long while, and then waits, like us. After a little while a Mexican-American shows up, to whom the Anglo says something in English. The Mexican-American turns towards us. "Are you painters?" he asks.

We all say that we are.

"We're going to see if that's true," he responds.

Then he has us follow him through some small passageways that seem like a labyrinth. We come to a storeroom and he gives each of us a can of paint and a brush.

"I'm going to give you an hour to prove that you can paint," he says.

Then he assigns each one of us a spot to work. Sure of myself, I immediately begin painting. After a while I see the foreman come by but I pretend not to see him, so that he'll think that I'm completely absorbed by my work. The frames I'm painting are coffee-colored and the walls, the color of cream. While making a big stroke, the bristles of my brush touch the wall, and I don't find any way to remove the spot I've made except to wipe it with my handkerchief. I'm not wearing a watch and I don't know if an hour has passed when I finish the job they gave me. A few minutes later, the Mexican-American appears, and he orders me to come down from my ladder. He sticks his hand into a pocket, pulls out a wad of bills and hands me five dollars.

"Thanks for coming, but you don't know how to paint," he

says.

I'd like to know why I was disqualified. But before I can ask any questions, he's gone, carrying the can of paint and the brush with him. I turn my head and look at the place I was painting and it doesn't look bad to me. I head out of the apartment complex, and in a minute, the Peruvian comes up to me, almost at a run. He was disqualified, too.

The Peruvian is a short man with Indian features, carelessly dressed, and he's wearing cowboy boots that are too big for his feet. We walk along an avenue looking for a bus stop or place to eat, because I haven't eaten all day. Every few seconds, the Peruvian says, "How bad life treats us, no?" I don't answer him because, after having lost the job, I'm in no mood to chat. But he keeps repeating, "How bad life treats us, no?" On the wall of a Chinese restaurant I see a sign that says, "All You Can Eat $2.60." I go in and the Peruvian follows me. I do exactly what the sign says. I grab a plate and fill it with fried rice and a little of each of the dishes that are in aluminum trays. A young oriental woman with long, straight hair tied in pigtails about halfway down her back, greets us from behind the glass of a counter. She looks at us with friendly, playful black eyes. Her cheekbones are prominent and her skin is tightly stretched across her face. Without changing her expression, she mumbles something that I take to be English. I don't understand a word of it, but I deduce that she's welcoming us, because we're the only diners in the restaurant. I smile to hide my ignorance and she goes away. I take out my phrase book and look for the way to ask for something to drink. Then I call her.

"Can we have some iced tea?"

I have learned to drink iced tea because it's not carbonated and it's cheap.

"Sure," she says. "Big or small?"

"Big one."

The Peruvian is surprised and he asks me how I learned to speak English. I show him my book and he says that he's going to buy one at his first opportunity.

While we are eating, he tells me that six months ago he left Peru, and crossed all of Central America illegally. In Nicaragua he was jailed for fifteen days. When he at last reached Mexico, in the state of Veracruz he found a job as a bricklayer's helper. He saved enough money to buy a bus ticket to Matamoros, on the border. Four times he crossed the River by himself, and four times he caught the train that goes north into the interior of Texas. *La Migra* caught him every time. Fortunately, he convinced them that he was Mexican, and each time they returned him to Matamoros. The fifth time he got through, and though he didn't know exactly where the train was going, he wound up in Houston. He met some Mexicans who let him sleep in their house for a while, but for three months now, he's been without steady work.

When the time comes to pay, I give the waitress the money that corresponds to my check, and she waits at the table for the Peruvian to pay. But he apparently doesn't intend to pay. He takes his drinking glass, which contains only ice, and raises it to his mouth, noisily chewing cubes.

"Pay your check," I tell him.

"Brother, I haven't got money," he says, humiliated. "I haven't worked and I haven't got any money. Will you pay it for me?"

"You should have asked that before sitting down to eat," I say, a little bit irritated. If I didn't have money to pay his part, the young woman would have to call the police.

While I pay, I ask him about the five dollars that they gave him for the hour he worked. He says that the driver of the car collected it when he saw the foreman paying him.

We return to the avenue, and while we're walking he keeps repeating the same phrase that I've by now heard too many times. Then he asks if, where I live, they can give him a chance to stay a few days while he finds work. I tell him that I'm in the same situation and may be thrown out myself.

"How bad life treats us, no?" I hear him say again. "One of these days, I'm going to Spain. People are probably more civilized there. Here, the people are ignorant. They don't know that for a man to survive, he's got to have help."

"You're right," I tell him.

Although I wouldn't be willing to make a trip to Spain, I recognize what the Peruvian says as the logic of the wetback. If luck isn't with you in one place, surely it will be better in another place. For the Peruvian, maybe going to Spain would be like going anywhere else, but I'm Mexican, and if one of these days I decide that my adventure in the United States is foolish, I've got the security of knowing that my country is only a bus ride away. When we reach the center of town, I say so-long to the Peruvian. He's looking for somebody to help him in the United States, and I can't be his friend.

LIKE FATHER, LIKE SON

There was nothing today at KLVL. Nothing as well on the corner. At noon my insides begin reminding me of my obligation to feed them. Coins rattle around in my pants pockets: pennies, nickels and a dime. I haven't spent them because you can't buy much of anything with small change. Even if they're no good, however, it hasn't crossed my mind to get rid of them. They feel a little bit heavy in the bottom of my pocket and make me remember that as bad as things are, I'm not yet, as they say, without a penny to my name.

Sometimes, when I look at the coins, they remind me of when my father went to Juárez, Chihuahua on a *bracero* trip. He and two townsmen had paid in advance for the services of a coyote whose job was to influence the authorities that picked *bracero*s to enter the United States legally as temporary agricultural workers. Three days after they'd paid the man, my Dad bought a newspaper just to have something to look at during the hours they spent waiting outside the contractors' offices. A picture he saw in the section of police reports alarmed him, and he called his two companions to have a look. The three looked at the photo of a cadaver lying on the ground. They immediately recognized the dead man, but they kept looking, trying to find an error. Finally, they decided that there was no cause for doubt. There in the newspaper was the name and photo of the coyote whom they'd paid three days earlier. The report said that three knife wounds had chilled him forever in the red light district.

The money they had wasn't enough for either hiring another coyote or for returning home. Soon they didn't have enough to pay the room in the boardinghouse where they were staying. Upon seeing them in such straits, the woman who owned the place softened her heart and let them sleep in a corner of her entryway. Their diet was reduced to tortillas with peppers in vinegar. On one occasion, they were able to buy only a bun of white bread. To keep from losing even a crumb, and so that all three would get an equal share, they cut it with a razor blade.

One of my father's companions fell ill after a few days. He was fevered and couldn't get up for days. They found little jobs here and there, like loading dirt into a truck. "What a bunch of stars we saw every time we lifted a shovelful," my father always said. A storekeeper gave them crates full of fruits that they carried through the streets, hawking at the top of their lungs.

"We had the look of beggars," my father would say with a bit of smile when he was telling the story to the family circle.

"Bad times," Mother would always comment.

She knew all the incidents in the travel tales that Dad told, and she hated to even hear *El Norte* mentioned.

"Sometimes we'd have good luck," Dad would narrate. "We'd go up to the buses that carried the guys who had been contracted as *braceros* and every time, somebody would notice our condition. 'We're going to something certain,' he'd say, 'so I'll leave you my food, I hope that you have good luck.' Then one window after another would open and so many guys would hand us paper bags of food that we couldn't hold them all."

"Those guys who were going wished us the best of luck, but we envied them," he'd add.

MOJADOS

Passing by a mechanic's shop, I see a group of four Hispanics talking and smoking in a leisurely way. In front of each of them is an open lunchbox and plastic plates containing the remainders of food. I ask them for work, but they say that they have no openings and can't tell me where I might find work.

"Gigs are scarce," one of them tells me. "But if you look, buddy, you're bound to find something."

"You should have come around a few minutes earlier. At least we'd have invited you to chow," another says.

Another one of them digs into his lunch pail and fishes out three flour tortilla tacos and offers them to me. They're made of eggs and canned beans.

"Why don't you go to the Church of the Virgin of Guadalupe. I hear that they help wetbacks find gigs," the first one tells me.

The church is only a few blocks away. It's an enormous building of red brick with mahogany doors and an ample yard covered with grass and flowers, and a big, paved parking lot. When I get closer I see that it is even bigger. Behind the church and to one side are other buildings of the same material. Everything seems quiet and deserted. I see only one man, who, to judge by his dress, probably isn't a doorman or servant. He's middle-aged, and he's leaning against one of the metal posts that hold up the asbestos roof of what looks like a carport. Both hands are stuck in his pockets, and his legs are crossed. He's wearing some old tennis shoes that once upon a time were white; they are tied with strings of a different color. He's tall and thin, and he's wearing a worn-out set of beige pants that are much too big for his size, along with a purple shirt that's much too tight. A muffler the same color as his pants is wrapped around his neck and mouth.

"Is it true that here they help wetbacks?" I ask him. I use the usual word in Spanish for wetbacks, *mojados*.

"Yes," he says from behind the muffler.

I see lots of doors but I don't see a sign telling me which one

70

to enter.

"In what way do they help?" I continue.

"They give away clothes, food at times, and they help you find work when there's opportunity," I hear him say. I note that his accent isn't Mexican, and I let him know.

"I'm Cuban," he says. "I'm an ex-pilot of the Cuban air force," he says proudly, perhaps hoping to give me a different impression of him, despite his clothing. "I belonged to the patrol squadron of Cuba," he continues.

"How did you get to the United States?" I ask.

He says that he was obsessed with coming to the United States and his profession gave him a way to make the trip. In one of his reconnaissance flights he changed directions and flew to an airport in New York. He felt sure that he'd get out of the Cuban plane and promptly be assigned to an American craft, but he was wrong in that respect. They received him at pistol point. He was jailed and was interrogated. After a great while they set him free, completely free. He came with nothing and they turned him onto the streets with nothing.

Since then, he's worked as a dishwasher, carwasher, janitor, gardener's helper, etc. He recalls his Cuban airplane with nostalgia, he says, while doing things like loading and unloading at warehouses. He's sorry he left and would like to go back to Cuba, but he knows that Fidel wouldn't accept him. But even now he won't accept his fate, and his pride has lately led him to decide that it's better not to work than to work at simple jobs, because, after all, he's a pilot.

"Where can I ask for help?" I say.

He points to some metal stairs that go up to a second story.

Upstairs is a small room divided into three sections with carpet on the floor. The gas heaters are burning and the temperature is welcoming inside. I sit in the waiting room in a comfortable overstuffed chair. Nobody is in view, but I'm in no hurry. Next to the chair is a table with aluminum legs and a glass top. Several magazines are lying on the table, and one of them shows a photo of Reagan raising his right hand with his palm extended, as if waving. Nancy holds him by the arm. But I don't open the magazine. I prefer to just take in the warmth of the room. In one corner there's a box of used clothing, but I don't bother with it, either. The denim pants and jacket that I bought when I arrived in Houston serve me well enough, because denim doesn't show dirt easily.

A sheet of glass divides an office from the waiting room. There's only space in the office for one desk and a chair. I don't see any books or bookcases, but stacks of papers are piled high on the desk.

To one side of the desk is a wall with a plywood door. I hear the voices of women talking.

The door opens and a tall woman of about thirty-five in a pale green dress appears. Her skirt comes down to her ankles, and her blouse comes up to her neck, where it's topped by a ribbon of white lace, just like the ends of her long sleeves. She has short hair tied tightly at the neck. Her bronze skin lets me know that she's Hispanic.

"Pardon," I say in Spanish, "is this the place where you help wetbacks?" As always I use the word *mojados.*

"*Mojados?*" she says to herself.

Some light wrinkles cross her forehead and her eyes look to the walls, as if she expected to find an answer there. Then she turns towards me with her eyes wide open, as if she was having trouble seeing. Her slight smile has vanished and now her lips are tightly shut. I feel her looking at me from head to foot.

"*Mojados?*" she repeats. This time it's clear that the query is directed at me.

"Yes," I say, baffled, "somebody told me that here you help *mojados.*"

"No!" she says with cold emphasis. "Here there are no *mojados.*"

Even more confused, I manage only to say thanks and to find my way down the stairs again.

The Cuban stands in the same position below, only now his chin is pressing the muffler against his chest. I tell him about the conversation I had upstairs.

"Undocumented worker is the correct term," he says.

HALLELUJAH!

When the sun goes down after a fruitless day, it's hard for me to return to my room. Only when I tell myself that I've got nowhere else to go am I able to start heading back. One night I casually pass by a church that's only a few blocks from my house. It's a Protestant church with high red brick walls and a sheet metal roof. As I walk by in the darkness, I see the parking lot, illuminated by big lights on the walls of the church. Cars that carry whole families are arriving. I decide that I'd rather see what they do than go home to my desolate room. The sanctuary is big and filled with well-finished cedar pews aligned in two rows beginning at the walls. The aisle between the two rows is carpeted in red and leads up to a pulpit that sits on a platform covered with parquet and about two feet higher than the rest of the room.

Everybody who comes in sees me sitting in the pew nearest the door. They greet me as if we knew each other. Before the sanctuary has filled, nearly forty groups have greeted me, always in the same way, "*Buenas noches, hermano,*" or "Good evening, brother." Electric instruments behind the pulpit begin scattering the notes of songs of praise. When the room is full, the pastor steps up to the microphone. The band goes silent. The pastor is of average height, with a bald pate, and he is fastidiously dressed in a suit of blue. He addresses the congregation, talking about the Lord in a paternal manner. In the congregation people shout, "Hallelujah!" Some of them, closing their eyes, lean their heads back and extend their arms outwards, mumbling something between their lips. Others stand up, almost immobile, and throw their heads back and put their palms on their chests. Others are kneeling and almost convulsing, with their heads against the backrests of the pews in front of them. The cry of "Hallelujah!" sounds on all sides, from voices that are choked with crying. The pastor doesn't quit talking. His voice is little by little gaining energy, while his hands now point at his flock or fly up towards the ceiling. As he comes to the climax of his sermon, his words are unintelligible, partly because he's

speaking rapidly and partly because the microphone emits deafening sounds. The shouts of "Hallelujah!," the sobs, the top-of-the
voice "Thank You, Lords," the shouts of the pastor and the elec-
tronic instruments—the band has resumed playing—all become
one. All of a sudden, the pastor and everyone else become quiet.
From among the congregation, people have come into the aisle on
their knees, slowly moving towards the foot of the pulpit where
the pastor awaits them with closed eyes, in silent prayer. When
the people on their knees reach the pastor, they spread out around
him. He lays his right hand upon each head, and with his fingers
extended, passes it above every one, pronouncing words that are
unintelligible to me.

Afterwards, an announcer says that Brother So-and-So is going
to come up to the microphone to tell how the Lord had been made
manifest in his life. A young man with a shirt considerably wider
than his thin frame rises to the pulpit. He says that the afternoon
before, he was running late for a visit with a family that had only
recently received the Lord into its house. The young man was late
because he had discovered that the shirt he had planned to wear
was missing some of its buttons. Desperate, he returned the shirt to
its hanger and looked among the rest of his clothes for something
else to wear. But all of his other shirts were dirty. He resigned
himself to wear the shirt with the missing buttons, and went back
to the hanger to get it.

"Would you believe, brothers?" he says, his eyes shining with
happiness and his mouth stretched into a smile. "The shirt now
had its buttons again!"

Everybody in the congregation lets loose a "Hallelujah!"

Then a middle-aged woman takes her turn. She says that two
days before she was terribly anxious because she didn't have money
to pay the rent. The next morning when her husband went to work,
she left the house and went to a coin-operated laundry. She put
her bundle of clothing into the machine, poured in a measure of
powdered soap, put a quarter in the machine's money slot, and
the machine began to operate. In her anxiety, she had forgotten to
close the top on the machine, and when it began to agitate dizzily,
two, one hundred dollar bills came floating into the air.

The congregation again explodes in shouts and praise.

At the end of the service, a short man with a round face and
short hair comes up to me.

"I've been watching you, brother, and I'm sure that I haven't
seen you join our service before. Our temple is open to everyone
who feels the necessity to come to the Lord in search of help."

"I've only come to see how you worship," I say.

"Can it be that you profess a different religion?"

"No, I don't have another religion. I've come here to ask if I can find help here. I've been without work and now I don't have money to pay the rent on the room where I'm living, and the rent comes due on Sunday."

"God has sent you to us, brother!" the man exclaims. "Nobody but God could have sent you to our temple, and you're certainly welcome."

He continues. "In your eyes I see the affliction that paralyzes your soul, but don't be afflicted because there's a reason why you have come to us. The Lord has sent you and we can't refuse anyone that He has sent. Here there is enough room for you to rest, even though perhaps not too comfortably. The important thing is that we have room. Here you won't lack for food, and even though it may not be the best, there's always something to put in your mouth. You should know that the Lord is just in all that He does. He sometimes punishes but he never forgets to provide food."

"Have you accepted Jesus as our only savior, have you accepted him in your heart?" he asks me.

Frankly, I don't know how to answer and he sees that immediately. He says that he, too, was distanced from Jesus a couple of years ago.

"Imagine," he says, "before, I wanted to become a boxer. Imagine that, will you! I had picked a career where you hit people, and the Lord doesn't like that. One day somebody spoke the word of God to me and I became aware of my error."

That guy talks to me for half an hour about his conversion, citing long passages he has memorized from a dog-eared Bible that he holds in his hands.

"If you are willing, I can help you so that Jesus, our savior, will live forever in your heart."

"I don't know how you do that," I answer.

"I already know that you don't know how, but that's exactly why He has guided you to us, to show you the road and how to follow it. Let's see," he says, "put your hand on your chest, bow your head and repeat after me."

I obey his orders and repeat word for word everything that he is saying.

At the end, he looks at my face and in the same way that someone would do who had finished a work of art, he backs off a little ways to contemplate his product. His face fills with a smile and his hands are still plastered to his chest and he exclaims, 'The affliction has been wiped from your face and in your eyes I now see the tranquility that only comes when Jesus reigns in our hearts. Our Savior!"

Nobody is left in the sanctuary, even though I can hear voices from behind the wall where we stand. The ex-boxer, satisfied with his labor, leads me into the yard of the temple, and from there we walk beneath the big lights on the building. On crossing a doorway, I see before me a big room with a concrete floor. A small portion of it is occupied by double-bed bunks placed against the walls. Each one is covered with sheets that aren't very white. Four other mattresses are stretched on the floor at the foot of one wall. Brown blankets are spread atop them. In the middle of the floor is a big table with two benches at its sides. Through another door is the kitchen, equipped with two, four-burner stoves, and a big aluminum tank that serves as a sink. Cooking utensils hang from nails in the walls and a lot of plates, glasses, pots and pans are stacked on top of a table and on a shelf beneath it.

When we return to the room of beds, a couple of guys are inside. One of them is about fifty years old, or at least, that's the impression his white hair gives, although his face doesn't seem as wrinkled as it should be at that age. He's a thin man of average height. The other I recognize immediately as the one who rose to the pulpit to tell the story of the buttons.

"The other brothers will be here later," the ex-boxing aspirant tells me. "You can stay here while you find work. A lot of undocumented people have come here. To us it doesn't matter if they are illegals or not. They stay for a few days and afterwards they go to other places or they find work and a place to live. Right now we don't have many guests, but sometimes we've had so many that we've gone looking for mattresses to give everybody a place to sleep."

Then the man says goodbye, reminding me to attend the service the following night.

I sit down on one of the benches by the table, joining the two men who are talking among themselves. They greet me, saying brother. I am new and their attention falls upon me. They ask where I come from, how I'm named, and everything that one is capable of asking when idle.

Afterwards, the young man with the oversized shirt tells his story. Just like the ex-boxing aspirant, he is a beginning preacher. The two dedicate themselves to knocking on doors, house to house, in search of souls to save. This guy says that he was once a member of a Pachuco gang in the neighborhood. He says he liked street fights, and to prove it, he unbuttons his shirt and shows us a scar on his back that runs from his shoulder to his waist. He says that the wound was about to take him to the other world, and that if the brothers of the congregation hadn't carried him to the hospital, he would have died, because his fellow gang members had abandoned him to his fate. He now says that he plans to become a preacher in Mexico.

The man with white hair isn't a preacher but he also begins to practice with me. I'm content to have found a place where I won't have to pay rent and food is free, and so I've got the patience to hear what they say. The white-headed man is from the state of Zacatecas and he wandered into the temple about a month ago, just like I did.

The ex-hoodlum goes into the kitchen and announces that he's going to prepare a pot of coffee. Meanwhile the white-headed man tells me how God has manifested Himself in his life. He says that once, while he was working on a construction job, a car had pushed him up against another car that was parked on the parking lot, and it would have squashed him had he not remembered God.

"In that instant I saw heaven," he says.

I am curious to know what heaven was like.

"All the houses and streets are of glass, completely illuminated," he responds.

"Couldn't it have been the impact that made you see stars?" I ask, knowing that he still hadn't made up his mind to become a preacher.

"Well, yes, it was the impact, but don't you know that God has his ways of making people see the truth?"

I don't contradict him. I ask how old he is and am dumbstruck when he says that he's not yet forty.

"Then why do you have white hair?" I ask.

"It's another story, nothing like the one I just told," he says. "It's because of something that happened to me that I wouldn't even wish upon my worst enemy. My hair was black before that happened, just five years ago."

The ex-hoodlum comes in with two steaming glasses of coffee and places them before us.

"Everybody takes me for an old man," the man from Zacatecas says after taking a sip from the glass of coffee. "Can you imagine how I won one hundred dollars and my hair turned white?"

I stay silent and he knows that I can't answer his question.

THE SNAKE

The man with the white hair tells me that five years ago he was taking care of cattle on a ranch near Lubbock.

"On the ranch were two houses, both of them wooden. One of them was well-built with gas stove, a refrigerator, furniture and a heater. The other was just a garage without a door. It had a dirt floor. I got used to sleeping in the garage during the summer, and only stayed at the house during the winter's cold spells.

"In the garage I slept in a kind of cot that I'd built myself. Three boards on top of a sawhorse, my bedroll and sheets. One night, I came in about dark, pretty tired because I'd had to rope and tie a steer to give him a shot in the navel. Before lying down, I'd drunk my usual cup of strong black coffee.

"I don't know exactly how long I was lying there without being able to sleep, with the sheet covering even my head. All of a sudden I heard a real light sound, like the snorting of cattle when they run into a weed that they don't like. But I had the feeling that the sound came from closer to me. Without taking the sheet off my head, I started listening real close.

"Meanwhile, I was trying to remember in detail everything that I had in the garage with me, even though I knew that nothing of mine was capable of producing that noise. All of a sudden, I heard it again. A chill went all through my body and stopped in my hair. I sat up in bed so quickly that I thought I'd surprise whatever it was, but I didn't see anything nor hear anything else. Everything was completely silent. The light from the moon filtered between the joints of the wood and lit up the room enough to see. My coffee pot was on the coals, and the embers glowed from time to time. For a minute I thought about getting out of bed to see if anything was knocking around outside the garage, but something told me to stay put.

"To tell the truth, I was afraid. My head felt swollen and my hair, like that of a porcupine, was standing on end. You have to remember that I'd been working in the same place for two years and that was the first time that anything had made me afraid. I sat for a long time, completely alert, but without even moving my head, for fear that I wouldn't hear the sound if it came again. I moved my eyes from side to side but nothing interrupted the silence. Not even the wind moved the weeds outside. I tried to convince myself that it had been a simple nightmare, but that argument did no good because I knew that I hadn't been asleep. Finally, I blamed my imagination, but I still couldn't stop feeling nervous.

"Tiredness got to me before daybreak, but I woke up about five in the morning, as was my custom. But this time I didn't get up. I stayed in bed until the sun rose high. I was still trying to find an explanation for my behavior the night before. When I leaned over to find my boots beneath the bed, I saw a track that came from the door and made curves until it got beneath my bed. I got goose bumps again as I told myself that a snake had visited me the night before. Then I noticed that there were really two tracks, one coming and one going. With the relief of someone who is out of danger, I said to myself that I'd been saved from snakebite. Three days earlier I'd swept the floor, and because there wasn't much dust, I couldn't tell just how wide the snake had been. A reptile, a serpent, a snake or whatever it was, it was the first time that I'd slept with anything like that beneath my bed.

"I went to work but I can't say I forgot about the incident. Instead, all the stories I'd heard from old people started running through my head. I vaguely remembered that someone had told me that, 'When a snake finds a comfortable place to sleep, it comes back.' Those words kept repeating themselves in my head until I thought I could see the dried lips of an old man telling me that. To my misfortune, that memory robbed my contentment.

"It wasn't agreeable to imagine myself sleeping with such a creature under my bed. Every few minutes I'd swear that I was going to sleep in the other house. Then I'd reproach myself for being so frightened by a little snake coming into the garage without asking permission. I even thought for a minute of quitting the job, but I immediately decided against it. When evening came, I was firmly resolved to give an exemplary punishment to the creature that had robbed my sleep. I should kill it, I decided. When I got to the garage, I made a big pot of coffee and put my shovel at the ready. A sure blow in whatever part of his body, I figured, would put him out of combat. Nervously, I waited. My hands sweated, but I guess that's normal because I was waiting to kill, not a rat, but a being that crawled on the ground and could well be poisonous. I was like a batter waiting for the pitch. My eyes were fixed on the doorway.

The wind wasn't blowing and I could hear even the slightest sound, and the moon gave me enough light to see. My behavior seemed exaggerated to me, and I told myself that maybe I had believed in something that wasn't possible or true, and that maybe what I thought I'd heard about snakes coming back had really been said about another animal. I was tempted to give up my position and go to sleep, but I was afraid to.

"Time gets long when you're waiting on something," the man with the white hair says while taking a couple of sips from his glass of coffee. "I was distracted for a few seconds by the fire whose coals glowed red around the coffee pot. When I looked back at the entrance what I saw left me paralyzed. A shout of terror stuck in my throat and left me with my mouth open. My blood seemed to clog my heart, which was beating desperately and hard. My head began to feel heavy and I felt my hair stand on end again.

"Fifteen inches of animal had appeared in the doorway. The head was bigger than a man's fist and it was followed by a body at least three inches thick, and it seemed to get bigger as it came into the garage. The shovel! I had it in my hand but that apparition had left me worse off than a statue. The beast—I can't call it by any other name—turned to one side, then the other, and when it seemed to notice my presence, I felt its sharp stare. I trembled. A heavy sweat soaked my whole body when I imagined that it was advancing on me.

"But no. It crawled calmly, like one who is in his own house, and before my bulging eyes, little by little I made out that its body was spotted brown, black and dark gray, that it was hefty and about seven feet long. Underneath my bed, after a little looking around, it slowly started curling up until it was only a circular bundle. By the time I realized that I had my shovel, it was too late. The beast had curled up right beneath the bedpost, and to make matters worst, its head was pointed in my direction. It was as if that terrible animal knew that I wanted to attack, but at the same time it knew that its stare would keep me frozen! That was a rude blow to the courage that I had felt at first. The most I was able to do was put my two hands on the shovel to hold myself up so that I didn't faint. Those eyes that flashed so evily in the half-darkness were dominating. I had never been in such a fix: I was in my own house, nailed down by the anmal's cold stare, and I was trembling from head to foot. Now I sometimes ask myself how far away I was from acting like those poor birds who, hypnotized by the stare of a snake, walk up to its waiting mouth. My shovel at that point was like a branch that kept me from falling into an abyss.

"The night advanced and I never knew if that beast was asleep or awake, because they don't close their eyes like human beings do. Very slowly I began to collect myself. I put myself on guard. My pot of coffee certainly had the warmth that my body needed, thanks to the coals, but I didn't have the valor to serve myself anything. The long hours I spent watching that animal and smothering my fear caused me moments of dizziness. A rustle in my bed put me on the alert about the time the sun started coming up. I saw the snake stretch part of its body with such precision that it was like a sword slipping out of its scabbard. It prepared to leave, stretching the rest of its body towards the door. As soon as its head was beyond the doorsill, I stood up and grabbed my shovel and a sharp pain hit me behind the knees. I felt like I was snapping my muscles, they'd been in one position for so long. I ignored the pain and managed to give the beast one good blow with the edge of the shovel, hoping to be done with it in one stroke. Its whole body trembled, and then it doubled and I saw it face-to-face. I felt like my hour had come, and I lost the composure that I had managed to regain. I started hitting it with the shovel without aim, not so much to kill it as to keep its head away from me, and most of the time, I was striking with the flat part of the shovel, not doing any damage. On the other hand, it was furious and full of courage and I felt its saliva splash my face as it showed me its open mouth. I could see the string of fine teeth threatening me and the tongue shaking itself inside the mouth. I didn't have time to quake. I threw blow after blow after that. Sometimes I managed to land blows on its head that made it bounce against the wall, but it shot back like a spring. I felt the rest of its body whipping my legs. I barely remember shouting sounds, as if I was fighting with another human being, but I don't know if I was insulting it or begging for mercy. During one of its movements, I tripped over its writhing body and fell on my back, landing halfway out of the garage. Man, fear can paralyze your body or give you great agility, either one! Because I'll tell you, as soon as I felt knocked down I was up on my feet, moving so fast I could never do it over again.

"How long did that last? I don't know. How did it plan to kill me? I don't know that either. It stationed itself with its head in the air and the rest of its body on the ground with the firmness of a man walking on two feet. Every time I managed to knock it down, it regained its position with a quick, convulsive movement, and that was when it whipped me with its long body. More than a couple of times it knocked me down, and once, I received a hard lashing on the forearm that put to sleep the fist in which I was holding the shovel. The beast's grotesque head came within inches of my face and had it not been for the handle of my shovel it could have bitten my neck, if that's what it wanted. In desperation, I gave it a long kick, and that would have been useless if my foot hadn't struck the wall of the garage. But then I had it with my foot pressing down on its neck, right beneath its head. It nearly slipped out and only with great difficulty could I force my arm, ignoring the pain, to push the blade of the shovel up against its neck. While I had it that way I was the victim of severe lashings, but I pulled together my strength and, putting one foot on a wing of the shovel, I pushed with precision and all the might of my back. Little by little, it quit lashing the ground. The tongue quit moving in its mouth. I had whipped it. I was bathed in sweat and dust, and I was breathing hard, as if I were about to explode. I laughed when I saw that terrible beast stretched out at my feet; tears came down my cheeks and mucous ran out of my nose. I was going crazy. For a long time I contemplated what to do, until I decided to burn it. I gathered up some firewood, sprinkled gasoline on it and set it on fire."

The white-headed man stayed quiet for a moment, lost in his own memories.

"I was several days in the hospital with my body swollen and bruised," he murmured.

"And the hundred dollars?" I asked.

"Well, that same day the owner of the ranch saw the head of the snake. It had toasted in a position that from a distance made it look as if it were still alive. The boss ran to his pickup and took out his rifle and was pointing it when I told him that there was nothing left to kill, but he took me for a fool and bet me a hundred dollars that the creature was alive."

RENT SUNDAY

Not long after the white-haired man told his story, the others came, seven of them, all Central Americans. The bunch of us prepare supper, which consists of scrambled eggs with *chorizo* and plenty of coffee.

The next day I don't go back to the services as the ex-boxer recommends. Instead, I pretend to be looking for work until late.

"The Lord has patience," the ex-boxer tells me.

When Sunday morning comes, instead of sitting in a pew, I sit in my apartment, waiting to tell the landlord that I can't pay the rent. About ten o'clock he shows up in his pick-up. He's wearing a thick cotton coat with a lining, a beret and a muffler.

"Today I'm going to give you back the key," I tell him.

"And why is that?" he says without giving it much importance. "Where do you think you'll live?"

"These last few days I've stayed at a church," I tell him.

"Are you going to become a preacher?"

"What preacher! I came here wet and I haven't been able to find work and in the temple I have a place to sleep. They give us food and sometimes people come with boxes of used clothing."

"So, you're a wet, huh? And without work," he says while thoughtfully eyeing his property. "A lot of wets have come lately, and they're mostly Central American."

"I'm Mexican."

"So you're coming from Mexico, eh?" he says to himself, as if in reality he were thinking of something else. "Tell the truth, how are things there? I like to ask because I'm Mexican, too, even if I live in the United States. How is it that the people all want to come to the north, and I who live here want to go live in Mexico again."

The landlord takes out a package of cigarettes. He offers me one, then takes one for himself, and then idly looks for his lighter in his pocket.

"We don't come here because we like it," I tell him, "we come to find work here to cover our needs at home, or simply to improve our economic situation. The only trouble is, it's not as easy as I thought. Since I came to Houston I've worked only an hour as a house painter."

"Well, it helps to know," he replies, "that you're not going to find life served on a silver platter as soon as you arrive. You have to struggle, and it isn't easy. For all you know, when you reach my age you won't come to collect rents from only a couple of doors, but from a whole apartment complex."

"That's a joke," I tell him good-naturedly.

"Who knows? Nobody."

Don Anselmo Mendoza breaks out in a smile, then laughs almost silently, letting go only a little whine. "Who would have believed," he says to himself, "Anselmo Mendoza giving good advice to a stranger who takes it well. I wish my sons would take it the same way."

Mr. Mendoza returns to his thoughts. He lights another cigarette and offers me one, too. He says that the house where my friend lives is his and that he has another one for rent. He also has another property, where he and his family live. At the house his wife and his four kids have a small green grocery that supplies a few small restaurants and also sells to the public.

He tells me that he came to the United States during the *bracero* period and worked sixteen years on a ranch in West Texas. During those years he managed to save some nine thousand dollars and, with the help of his boss, he became a legal resident. In 1970 he moved to Houston and was able to buy a house with his savings. For several years he worked as a bricklayer by day and as a watchman at night. In his free time and during slack periods in the construction business, he took his station wagon to farms north of the city, where he bought fruits and vegetables that he sold door-to-door and to small restaurants. His business grew until he didn't have to peddle anymore.

He brags that in his native town in Chihuahua, where he has had a concrete house built, his townsman call him Anselmito the Millionaire. But his voice changes rapidly when he talks about his sons. He becomes grave and hesitant.

"A lot of times I've asked myself," he says with the expression of a man with regrets, "who it is that has done such damage to my sons? Is it me for being weak of character? Is it my wife for having spoiled them all of their lives? Or is it this country? I don't know what it is, but something has certainly harmed them."

His sons, except for the youngest, who is barely twelve years old, have dropped out of school. They haven't married, and though they have taught themselves to be mechanics, they only work when they want to. The youngest son, Don Anselmo says, shows signs of following in his older brothers' footsteps. Mr. Mendoza says that when he's tried to correct his sons, they've answered him in English, which he's never really mastered. His wife usually defends them, even knowing that they are wrong. He tells me about an incident in which he arrived at the house with the station wagon full of produce that he'd bought. He began to unload the boxes and baskets, carrying them into the storeroom that is in front of his house. Meanwhile his sons were watching television on a sofa in the living room. None of them offered to help. Just then the phone rang; a client was asking for a delivery. After taking down the order, Mr. Mendoza returned to unloading while his sons continued watching television. When he tried to reproach them for their indolence, they got up and went into their rooms without responding to a word he said.

"I have continually repented of having come to the United States," he says. "In Mexico, at least in the countryside, where people are humble, my sons would have become useful young men, not what they are now, men without a profession, even though I have offered to support them if they want to study. For the rest of my days," he says, while the wrinkles in his face grow deeper, "I'm going to live in Mexico with my wife. But before that, I believe I'll sell everything I have, because if I leave it to them, I'm sure that they'll waste it. They don't know how hard it is to make money and so that they can learn, I'll have them start from the bottom."

The matter of my rent now seems forgotten. Before leaving, he hands me his card and he says that so long as I can't find a better job, he'll give me work to do in his fruit and vegetable business.

It's the first time I've heard that kind of offer since I came to Houston.

"I haven't been doing anything but waiting for a job, small as it may be, and if you want, I'll start right this minute," I tell him.

"Today is Sunday and it's not Christian to work today. Or are you maybe not Christian? I'll wait for you tomorrow at my house," he says.

Early the next day, I present myself at his house. It's located on a piece of land about fifteen yards wide and thirty yards long. Three buildings are located on the grounds. At the base of the property is a carport with a metal roof. The area beneath it is stained with oil and stacked with motor parts. It's the garage where

Don Anselmo's sons do their work. To the side of it is another
house, apparently vacant, and small, about fifteen yards square. A
wooden landing leads up to its second story. The third building is
a bigger place where Don Anselmo, his wife and children live. Up
against the street in what looks like an addition to the house is the
green grocery Don Anselmo operates.

My job is easy. I help Mr. Mendoza carrying boxes and baskets.
I pick out the products that are in poor condition, and place them
aside, and I clean the place. My first payday is Saturday. Don
Anselmo gives me one hundred dollars.

I pass one, two, three weeks this way, and my only entertainment is to go to the movies or to dance with the *ficheras*, or taxi
dancers, who work in bars in the neighborhood, charging a dollar
a dance.

After a month at the green grocery, I've made a few dollars,
but in spite of them, Houston is for me a hopeless city, or more
precisely, I have lost faith. My friend hasn't been able to turn up a
job for me, as he thought he could, and I can't keep putting myself
in debt. Nor can I hope that Don Anselmo will ever give up his
vegetable business to me, and sometimes I feel like he's hired me
for sentimental reasons, not because I'm needed. I can replace the
labor of his wayward sons, only so long as they don't care to work.
And outside of that, I'm know there's no hope in Houston. I have
for examples young men like Chesperito, who I have seen drag his
misery to the corner, feeding himself with what they give away in
the mission; the woman who came with the child in her arms to the
radio station, more, it seemed, to get in out of the cold than with
any real hope of finding a job; Abel, who despite his determination,
remains without steady work; and the old man in black gabardine,
who almost certainly will end his days in nostalgia for his youth
in Mexico. The attitude of the Peruvian makes more sense to me.
I'm going to leave Houston, but not for Spain. When I talk over
my plans with the friend who invited me here, he says, "at this
point, I can't blame you a bit."

I also tell Don Anselmo that I plan to leave. He gives me an
extra day's pay.

"Maybe one of these days, I'll get to go to Mexico, even if it's
only for a vacation," he says.

"If that's the case, can I give you some advice?" I answer him.

"What is it?" he says.

"Hang on to your billfold."

SAN ANTONIO

On the day that I arrive in San Antonio, I've got less than one hundred dollars in my pocket. There's a cloudless sky above, and it's sunny, but not hot. I know that the first thing that I should do is look for a place to stay, but I feel a little drowsy from the trip and so I instead go into the bus station's waiting room for a while. I sit down in a chair to which a television is attached, and I deposit 25 cents according to the instructions. The apparatus swallows my money and doesn't work. I content myself with smoking a cigarette.

The noise of video games and the shouts of their players fill the whole room. The Chicano sitting in chair next to me makes comments in English to his television set, as if the actors were listening. Over the loudspeaker system, somebody announces, first in English and then in Spanish, the impending departure of a bus.

On going outside I find myself facing a line of taxis, parked along the curb.

"Where are we taking you, young man?" says a Hispanic with a fat double chin from inside his taxi.

I look from one side of the street to the other. There are a multitude of advertising signs, and that tells me that I'm in San Antonio's downtown district. I walk to the corner and see that right across from the bus station is a hotel, but because of its elegance I don't even bother to ask the price of a room.

"I need to find a place to stay," I tell the taxi driver.

"Climb in," he says. "I'll take you right now, just tell me where it is."

"I don't know where it is, I need to find one."

"Well, I'll help you find one, right now."

The cabbie looks at me and perhaps noting my indecision, more to affirm than to ask he tells me, "You're coming from Mexico, right?"

"Yes, and how much are you going to charge me?"

"Seven dollars."

"Seven dollars," I repeat, more to myself than to the driver. Meanwhile I look down the street, looking for a sign that says Hotel. Seven dollars seems like a high price to me. This isn't the first time I've hired a taxi, but I've never paid more than three dollars before.

When I'd gone to the bus station in Houston I'd stood in front of the sign that announced departures and prices and calculated that after paying the fare, I'd be left with less money than it takes to survive for a week living on hamburgers and fried chicken. Seven dollars represents a day's meals.

A white man comes out of the waiting room dragging a huge suitcase. The Chicano cabbie heads towards him, talking in English. The white man says thanks, but he doesn't stop. A car stops suddenly at the opposite sidewalk and a young blonde, tall and thin, gets out and runs towards the white man, embracing and kissing him.

"Climb in, *paisano*," the cabbie insists, eyeing my indecision again. "I'll take you right now."

It occurs to me that the driver, might possibly be like the majority of Mexican cabbies, who, on seeing that one doesn't know a city, take the opportunity to make big money. A few hours remain before sundown, and I'm in hopes of saving some money.

"Thanks," I tell the driver, "but first I'm going to walk for a while."

Among the people passing through the bus station, I note not without surprise that I'm not the only person who has chosen this city. It only takes an instant for me to recognize the others, and they also recognize me. It's as easy as if each of us were wearing a sign saying "Wetback." Maybe it is because we're from the country and have a walking style that comes from being used to encountering rises and dips in our path. Or maybe it's the accessories we wear: jeans with horseshoes or heads of horses embroidered on their back pockets, the same as on the collars of shirts, on hats, or on big, flashy belt buckles. In some but not all of the wetbacks I encounter, I've noted a reserved attitude, like that of a person who knows he's not on his home turf.

From time to time we greet each other with a movement of the head, as if saying, "How are you doing, buddy? You, too, are here?"

Stores suceed one another for block after block. On turning a corner, I set eyes on the tower of San Antonio, a concrete column that's taller than many buildings. Afterwards people will tell me that several men have had the courage to throw themselves from its heights, staining the cement walkways with their bodies. Those men must have been familiar with the legend of Icarus, who wanted to reach the sun by flying on wings of wax. As Icarus was getting close, the sun melted his wings and he had to return to earth, against his will. Those who've jumped from the tower have surpassed his idea. After hitting the sidewalks, they've been able to reach the sun, and even go beyond.

A canal of water snakes through the center of the city, a river that perhaps was once an *arroyo* that the San Antonians have made into a concrete channel with sidewalks and thick, varied vegetation on both sides. They call this the Paseo del Río, or River Walk, but the day is so cold that I decide not to take a walk along its banks.

Not far from the center of downtown I find a hotel that appears to be inexpensive, or to be more exact, that looks old and neglected. As soon as I step inside what might be called the lobby, a rancid odor hits my nostrils. In one corner, behind a dark glass built into a counter, a head without much hair sticks itself into view. Upon sensing my arrival, it slowly twists a little, like the head of a toy clown in a box whose spring has grown tired. Its face is pale and thin.

"Yes, sir?" it asks, from behind eyeglasses that make the eyes seem larger than they are.

I ask about rooms and the head tells me that yes, there are vacancies, at five dollars a day. The man takes a notebook out of a drawer and lays it out in front of me. From his shirt pocket he takes a pen and asks my name. The rancid odor bothers me and I say that I'd first like to see a room. A little disappointed, he puts his pen upon the notebook and points towards a stairway at the foot of the lobby.

The wooden stairs creak beneath my feet. I come to a second floor and find a large hallway whose floor is covered with a narrow carpet. The stink is stronger here. I hear a man and a woman talking to one another from one of the rooms. Several of the doors are open. From what I can determine, apart from the couple, there are no guests. I lean into one of the rooms, and despite the light from a bulb, it seems to remain in shadows. There's a metal bed whose varnished finish still shines. Tinged sheets cover a mattress so deformed that it looks like somebody might have pulled the stuffings out. On the bathroom wall is a mirror whose reflective surface has darkened.

On returning downstairs, I find the old man with his pen and notebook ready to write down my name. But I tell him that I'm not going to rent a room. He doesn't say anything. He just goes back behind the counter.

I pass by a Holiday Inn, a Hilton and similar others in whose entrances are stationed uniformed bellboys, ready to assist the client in every way. Guests drive up and the bellboys run to their cars, greeting them and bowing to show humility. The guests open their trunks without getting out of their cars, the bellboys pick up the suitcases, and with an air of dignity, carry them back to the entrances taking short, forced steps. I imagine that a room in one of those places would cost me what I've budgeted for the week.

Finally, I come upon a hotel that isn't luxurious but is clean, where guests share a common bath and shower room. The price is only forty dollars a week.

THE WEST SIDE

As in Houston, I begin walking the streets in search of work. My hopes come to rest with restaurants, and a job as dishwasher. I walk without any direction in mind and drift into the Latin quarter, El West Side, as they say. Later I'll learn that it doesn't matter how you say that, it always means the same thing. Here in San Antonio, every skin color has its assigned direction. The North Side is for the whites, the East Side for the blacks, the West Side for the bronze-skinned, and the fourth or South Side, I never figure out. I suspect that the South Side is Hispanic, too, because people tell me that Hispanics are a majority in San Antonio, but it might also be a side of town on which the races have begun to mix.

The neighborhood is a succession of wooden houses, some older than others. Some are nearly at the point of falling down. Only voices or noise from sound equipment bear evidence that they're still occupied. Other houses are well-preserved, carefully repainted, with yards of grass, flowers and well-trimmed shrubbery. Along the street it's rare to find a house that doesn't have a car parked in front, though some of the cars are obviously not in running condition.

I hear a song from the 'fifties playing from inside a car of the same epoch. The volume is so much higher than the noise of the motor that I can hear the music from a block's distance. The old car is luxurious, shiny and painted in an unusual way. At first glance it looks like it is engulfed in flames from its front to its mid-section. On the trunk the figure of a svelte Indian woman is painted, with firm busts and legs. She is walking upon some rocks into a strong wind, which makes her long black hair undulate like a flag at high mast. On the rear windshield is a decal of a Hispanic man wearing a black derby, black eyeglasses and a black Mexican-style moustache. The car has shiny rims and it is slung so low that it almost drags the pavement. A Chicano with short hair carefully combed back is driving it. He is accompanied by a young woman whose face is covered with make-up. Her gaze is fixed towards the

91

front and the cold wind that comes through the vent window plays
with her hair.

Later, I'll encounter other people like them. They are Low Riders, those of the old but good cars, those of the old but good music.
Their manner of dress reminds me of a picture of my grandfather
that my parents have in a room of our house. The same type of
hair, combed back. Loose-fitting pants, with pleats and blousing
legs, suspenders, and a similar shirt, buttoned to the top button.
The only difference is in the footgear: my grandfather wore rough
sandals, while the Low Riders wear shiny shoes.

Technology has made trains obsolete, just like oxen, and on
the West Side idle tracks stretch out in parallel lines for blocks
on end. Old trackside offices are abandoned, too. A big office
building with thick walls is almost covered with overgrowth. Only
openings remain where once there were windows and doors. On
the inside there is nothing but rubble and dried dog feces. To the
side of the house is a two-story building, occupying most of a block.
Its window panes are shattered and in their places, thin sheets of
wood have been placed, and the building has been marked with
the weak warning that entry is prohibited. Two hotels remain, one
on each side of the building, each with its respective lounge. I go
into the first. Its only customers are a couple of Hispanics about
fifty years old, with red faces, seated together on stools in front
of the bar, each of them contemplating a bottle of beer in silence.
The bartender is a Hispanic of about the same age who, despite
the worn condition of his clothing, has made an effort to present a
clean appearance.

"What will I serve you? A beer?" he asks in a mixture of
English and Spanish.

"A good, cold one," I say, sitting down on a barstool.

He hasn't exaggerated the coldness of the beer. He gives me a
bottle in which pieces of ice are floating.

The three men begin chatting in a mixture of English and Spanish. The bartender says he's tired of his job, but brags that he can
uncap a bottle and slide it down the bar to the exact spot where the
customer is sitting. In one corner the juke box waits for someone
to drop in a coin. Its lights flash in changing patterns, as if it were
anxious to sing. The bartender and his friends begin gossiping
about someone.

The bar has a second or back room, bigger than the first, where
half a dozen billiard tables sit. A half-dozen men are seated in
there, and also an extremely thin woman. Her skin and hair seem
mistreated. She sits with her bony legs crossed, and thin hands

atop her knees. Looking at her from the side, I can tell that she was attractive in her better years. She is dressed in pants of a cheap fabric and in a black t-shirt. One of the customers walks up to her, puts one hand on her waist and another on her fleshless rear end, saying something in English. She looks at him with indifference.

When I leave the bar, I see a younger, more buxom woman, dressed in tight white pants and a thick cotton sweater, passing by on the sidewalk outside. I watch her swing her hips with every step. The signs that say Hotel catch my eye. I am tempted to offer her the money I've got in my pocket, but then I recall that I've got to survive. I catch up with her, say good afternoon, and tell her that we'll see each other one of these days, but she doesn't take me into account.

Further up the street, I come to an avenue sustained on high by thick concrete pillars that form an arc whose extremes pass from one side to the other of the forgotten railroad neighborhood and its bars. Beneath the freeways life is much different than above.

THE DREAM

For several days I take city buses completely by chance. I stand at bus stops and board the first bus that comes along. Sometimes the buses have taken me to neighborhoods where the houses are luxurious and new, presumably, where white people live. Everything is clean in those areas, and the streets are quiet, far from the tumult of downtown. Having nothing to do in those neighborhoods, I've stayed on the bus.

After a few days of not finding work, I begin to feel desperate and to lose faith, and for moments, I've been at the point of asking where I might find a mission, like those in Houston. But I've always recovered my spirits quickly, telling myself that the city is big and there's a lot of it that I haven't seen yet.

One night about daybreak, I sit up in bed and with great relief discover that I am in the same bed, with the same coverings, between the same four cream-colored walls of the hotel. In a dream, I had arrived at my village in conditions that I dread. I saw myself crossing the main street. I was carrying a bundle of clothes and an atrocious hunger that was devouring my intestines and making noises so loud I was afraid they'd denounce my presence. I was also carrying the bitter knowledge that I'd failed in my venture to the United States. I was nearing my parents' house. I could see the red adobe walls and tin roof of the main part of the house and of the kitchen, a separate structure. Everything was silent, and not even a dog was waiting in the yard to announce my arrival. From the chimney a string of smoke rose into the air, and with wavy movements kept rising up until it became invisible in the air. The smoke signified that my mother was preparing tortillas. It was about eleven o'clock in the morning, and at that hour, there's nothing else she could be doing. I was sure that it was her because I am completely familiar with her daily activities. They've always been the same, all of my life. She rises about five in the morning to wash the *nixtamal* that she's boiled the night before, and afterwards she takes it to the mill that is the center of the village.

94

On her return, she makes a fire in the hearth and starts boiling the water for a pot of coffee for my father, who has to go to work, and my brothers, who have to tend to the animals and then go to school. After that she prepares a lunch to take to my father and for my brothers to eat when they come home from school. Then she cleans the house and begins to make tortillas.

In my dream I was coming to my parents' house, but I didn't feel any kind of happiness, as on other arrivals, because this time I was arriving with nothing. I approached with slow steps, like someone going to an unknown place, but the truth is, I didn't want to arrive.

At the entrance to the house, the little pine trees had grown, a bush was in flower, and the sugar cane had shot up beneath the water faucet. Our carpentry shop was quiet, perhaps because there had been no orders, and Dad was devoting himself to other labors. All of a sudden, I heard my name and I recognized the voice calling it as that of my Mother. She had seen me from behind the screen that covers the kitchen window. Immediately she came out of the kitchen door towards me, repeating my name with happiness painted on her face. She walked swiftly, while drying her hands on an apron stained with corn. I smiled, too, trying not to show my empty hands, and I, too, took hurried steps towards her. She embraced me, still repeating my name and saying that she was happy to see me.

"I couldn't bring you anything," I said, trying to explain the miserable bundle that I carried beneath my arm. But she paid no attention to my excuses and kept saying that she was happy to see me return home. We went into the kitchen and were met by the smell of something burning; she had left a tortilla cooking on the *comal* and it had burned to charcoal.

"I couldn't bring anything, *Jefa*," I kept trying to explain. "*La Migra* caught me and I couldn't bring anything."

I was telling that lie to my Mother when I woke from my sleep. I got up and looked around the room slowly, like a person who has just arrived after a long absence. I looked out the window and saw that it was daylight; the sun was hidden beneath the tall buildings.

"It was only a dream," I told myself aloud. It was time to get out in the street and look for work again.

THE PRINTING PLANT

On my return from looking for jobs one afternoon, I come upon a building that is only a concrete box, at whose sides several cars are parked. Noise is coming out of the building. Going up close to it, I lean inside a big door whose metal curtain is raised. The noise that I hear is coming from two rows of machines whose gears are in rapid motion. The inside of the building is spacious, with a metal roof and several skylights. Huge rolls of paper are stacked atop one another, in columns that reach to the ceiling. Here and there are stacks of newly printed newspapers. About a dozen men in blue work uniforms come and go from the machines, shouting and making hand signs, some men giving orders and others obeying. On their shirts are two patches, one of which carries the name of a printing company, and the other, the last names of the workers. A couple of fork lifts move about between the machines and the walls, carrying rolls of paper and stacks of newspapers. A fine dust, the product of all this activity, floats in the air. I sit down on the threshold to watch.

A young man pushing a hand truck loaded with ink-stained stacks and barrels of paper goes towards the building's exit. He's making his way with difficulty towards a big steel trash bin on the parking lot. When he reaches the trash bin, he rests for a moment, looks at the bin, which is taller than he is, and then looks at the mountain of trash he's dragged out of the building. He's short, with hair coming down to his shoulders. I watch him struggle to raise a barrel of trash up to the mouth of the bin. He tries to lift it to his shoulder but its weight makes him stagger. I hear him curse the barrel, but even that doesn't help. Finally, he gives up and begins taking the trash from the barrel and throwing it into the bin by handfuls.

I offer to help him. He looks at me strangely but doesn't say anything. Between the two of us, we lift the vile barrel of trash and easily pour its contents into the mouth of the bin.

"Are you a *mojado*?" he asks after saying thanks.

"Yes," I tell him. "I'm looking for work."

"We're short a clean-up man. Right now I'm the only one and the job is for two," he grumbles.

Then he points to the place where the offices are located.

Behind a glass door is a hallway with mosaic tile. Several doors open into the hallway. I go into the first door that I find open. Inside are two desks behind which two young women are typing. One of the women is blonde and chubby, the other a little bit thin and bronze-skinned.

I say hello to get their attention. The blonde is closest to me. She asks me something in English, and I say that I'm looking for work and that someone told me that the company needs a janitor. She is left with her mouth open, and me, mute. She hasn't understood a word of what I told her. I try to attract the attention of the other woman, whose bronze skin tells me that she might speak Spanish. The two look at each other while I stand there, silent and nervous. They say something to each other in English. By the way they look at me, I guess that they think I'm lost.

"Can I help you with something?" the bronze one at last says in perfect Spanish.

I repeat in Spanish what I'd told the blonde in English.

"Just a moment," she says.

She gets up from her desk, goes down the hall and disappears into an office.

The blonde returns to her work. I am full of hope. I tell myself that this is the way things happen. All of a sudden, when you're least expecting it, you get what you were looking for. Every few seconds the blonde looks up and smiles at me, perhaps to calm my nerves. I walk up and down, running my fingers through my hair. I look at the floor, at the ceiling and at the vacant desk of the bronze-skinned woman.

A few minutes later she appears at the foot of the hallway. I look at her face, trying to discern what kind of news she brings me, but I'm not able to determine anything. She doesn't make any sign, I suppose, because after all, I'm only a person who has come to ask for something. On seeing her walk through the hallway I have the impression that she is modeling her tight pants and a t-shirt bearing the face of Michael Jackson. As she passes one of the open doors, somebody speaks to her and she smiles, but doesn't stop. The most striking parts of her beauty are her breasts. They make Michael Jackson wobble like a dancing puppet.

She comes to me smiling and saying that she's going to give me an application to complete. She points me towards a chair while she goes to her desk and takes a yellow sheet out of its drawer. She gives it to me right away.

Both sides of the sheet are filled with questions in English and Spanish. I don't think I have what could be called an address—nowhere permanent, anyway—and the Social Security number I list, of course, is false. I turn the sheet over without knowing what to do. The bronze-skinned woman reviews the data that I've noted on the form.

"When do you want to start work?" she asks.

Her words echo inside my head like something that I had long ago only imagined I had heard. But I want to believe they're real.

"Immediately!" I tell her.

LA MOTA

In the printshop I take the place of the Vampire, the nickname of the guy who I helped to dump the trash. They put him to work as a "catcher" of the printed papers that the machines vomit out at great speed.

My co-workers welcome me by insisting that I buy a twelve-pack of beer to drink after work. In response to their questions, I tell them that I'm from the state of Oaxaca.

"Oaxaca? Oaxaca! The state of good pot!" exclaims Javier, a Chicano whom they call Little Ox, whose brother, known as Ox, also works on our shift. Both of them say that they were once *coyotes* who operated out of Nuevo Laredo. After a while, the Mexican police got tired of them, and the Ox had to spend several weeks in jail. In jail he learned to talk like a Mexican, and in our vocabulary, ox is a minor insult when used instead of a name. He'd come out of jail saying, "Listen, ox," "Look, ox," "How are you, ox?" "Yes, ox," "No, ox," "Go ahead, ox," and such things, and because of that, the Chicanos decided to name him the Ox.

"Do you grow *mota*?" Javier asks me. *Mota* is slang for marijuana, like "pot," "grass" and "weed."

When I say no, they laugh as if they don't believe me.

"Well, you sure have the face of a pothead," Javier says.

They all concur in the observation.

"It's because there's no need to grow it," I tell them, lying to satisfy their curiosity. "Down there, growing it means you have to deal with smugglers, but if you go to a farmworker and ask him for a little weed, he'll take a bunch of it out of a basket and give it to you. We've got no need to go around smoking seeds like you guys do," I boast.

"Here, a baggy costs you twenty dollars," says George Sánchez, the chief of our shift. "And that's just an ounce."

"There a kilo costs you five hundred pesos," I tell him.

Everybody starts calculating, transforming Mexican pesos to dollars and kilos to pounds. It turns out that marijuana would cost about thirty dollars a pound, if its price were in line with the figures I imagined. They all say that someday they'll go to Oaxaca to buy some.

"And that's nothing compared to the mushrooms of María Sabinas of Huatla Jiménez," I say to impress them, though in reality I don't know the town, much less the infamous María Sabinas.

"María Sabinas!" exclaims Javier, who seems to be the most experienced in matters of drugs. "The queen of mushrooms, that crazy woman."

Then he tells how he and a friend once tried mushrooms and that the last thing he remembered was his friend wanting to throw himself off a bridge because he believed that the trees beneath were calling him. The other workers listen to this story with enthusiasm, and they begin making vague plans to go to Oaxaca.

"But you've got to be careful," I warn them, "because some *gringos* have been to Huatla de Jiménez and they've gone into the mountains looking for mushrooms by themselves. One of them died because he ate poison mushrooms. Another one of them fell off a mountain—or was pushed—and the third got bitten by a rattlesnake. All because they didn't consult María Sabinas."

MY ROOM

As soon as I can, I check out of the hotel, whose room was costing me half of my salary. I find a second-story room in the house of some elderly people, to whom I arrange to pay fifty dollars a month. The room has a bed, for which the landlady provided me with a pair of white sheets and a pillowcase, a table that was once a part of a grand dresser, with its respective chair, and a closet. The sheetrocked walls were once certainly white, but they've turned yellowish, and there are spots in the corners where rain water has leaked in. The floor is covered with an old rug. Out of the windows I can see two streets, because the house is located on a corner. The house and its property are surrounded by a chain link fence.

The landlord lives on the first floor, but I see him only a few times shortly after sunrise, when his wife, who must be more than sixty years old, takes him out in the entryway, in his overcoat, and seats him in a rocking chair to watch her perform her domestic duties. At night, the two lock themselves in, and you don't hear anything more than the sporadic murmur of a radio or television. I've never exchanged more than formalities with them, coming and going, except on the day that I rented my room, when the landlady asked me my name.

"Sainted Virgin!" she exclaimed on hearing it, pressing her palms to her breast. "Just yesterday a man with the same name as you shot himself in the head with a pistol."

My star-crossed namesake had lived in the house next door. His old house, nearly abandoned when he lived there, now had no owner, for he had no relatives to inherit it. He didn't even have a dog to bark for him.

"What a coincidence," was all I could say.

"The state will probably keep the house," she ventured.

The quiet of the house and the loneliness of my room contribute to depression, and that's why I've bought some posters for its walls. Above my bed is one of a dark-skinned woman who seems to be have been drawn, or maybe chiseled. She's tall and

101

thin, with rounded thighs with hips born from the waist of an ant.
She smiles at me inexhaustably. On another wall I've hung a poster
of a skeleton dressed in denim, who is riding through a cemetery
at night on a motorcycle. Riding behind him is a bronze-skinned
woman with her feathered arms raised upwards, forming a kind of
aureola around them. Her big, round busts are bare to the wind,
and her eyes glow in the darkness. These nighttime travelers are
moving, more than upon the ground, upon a purple cloud set in a
dark blue sky. The light of the moon creeps around a black cloud,
giving the woman's body a silver glow. On a third wall is a picture
of a cowgirl brandishing a rope.

THE WOMAN IN THE STREET

I work from three in the afternoon until eleven at night. One night when my shift ends, I have a few beers with my co-workers in the parking lot. Afterwards, I decide not to accompany them on their rounds to bars on the West Side. I decide to go home, walking as usual.

Two blocks before arriving at my apartment, I run into a woman about thirty years old. As I pass her, I hear her sobbing. She's short and a little chubby and wearing jeans and a blouse whose color I can't make out in the darkness. The street is deserted, save for an occasional passing car. On sensing my nearness, she calls out and I go up to her.

"Take me with you!" she blurts out.

Her request perplexes me. I try to take a good look at her in the dim street lighting. Her face is round and her hair, which falls to her waist, is disheveled. She isn't pretty, but she isn't very ugly, either. I've rarely had a woman ask to go anywhere with me, especially not with tears in her eyes. I've only got a single-sized bed, but she's not very fat, and I'm not either. I recall the times that I've had to hire prostitutes over by the railroad tracks, and I feel lucky. Here I am standing before a woman who voluntarily wants to go with me.

"Well, let's go," I say.

"No, not just like that," she says, still whimpering.

"Well, I've got a few dollars, how much do you want?"

"I'm not one of those," she says, a little irritated. "I live over there," she says, pointing to the house across from us. "I have a car, television, a stereo and clothes that I want to take with me. Help me get them and I'll go with you wherever you want."

It's not such a bad proposition, but I know that to go into somebody else's house and take things is risky, even with the consent of someone who lives there.

"I want to leave my man," she says, clarifying the situation. "And right now he's not home."

103

Then she pulls out a handful of keys and shows them to me, telling me which one is for the house and which for the car.

"I'm not going into the house with you. If you want to go with me, go the way you are. Forget about your things," I tell her.

She insists that she bring her things and tells me again that her man isn't home. I refuse to go along with her plan and tell her so-long.

"Please," she stubbornly says, grabbing me by the arm. "Come on, here are the keys!"

I begin to have doubts. Maybe she knows what she is doing. Instead of letting go of my arm, she pulls me towards her house and, like an imbecile, I let her lead me on. She gives me the keys, again showing me the one that goes to the house. We go around the house, making a U, until we come to a door. She opens the screen door and tells me to put the key in the lock of the inside door.

I open the door and look in. Nobody is inside.

"Wait for me a minute while I go get some things," she says, disappearing into an adjoining room. She opens a closet and takes out clothes that she stacks on a bed. Every few seconds, without stopping her motions, she looks over at me, and it seems that her look says that I should keep waiting. I stand inside the door, wondering how I could have been so bold as to have entered the house with her.

All of a sudden, the door opens from outside and a man with his eyes wide open stands before me. He immediately throws a blow which glances off my cheek, then comes at me, trying to grab hold of my neck and bellowing something about why I came into the house. He isn't any bigger than me and, like me, he seems startled. I pull him away from neck, and try to return the greeting that he gave me when he came in.

The woman has begun crying and she doesn't answer the questions that he shouts at her. He leaps off to the kitchen and puts his hands into the sink, rattling spoons and forks without taking his eyes off of us. I see him take out a big knife, about six inches long.

I open the door and jump down the four steps of the front porch, but the yard is wet. I slip and fall. I get up, start running and cast a glance behind me. He's running behind, the knife blade glinting in the dim street lighting. He's yelling for me to stop, but I've got nothing to say to his knife, and I keep going as fast as if I were flying. I come to my house, leap up to my door and look back again. I don't see him. I manage to find the key to my room, go in and, without turning on the lights, lie down panting on my bed, my eyes glued to my window. Not more than a minute has passed when I see two cars rolling slowly down the street, each with four passengers aboard. In the second of the cars somebody is shining a flashlight into the bushes and shadows at the sides of the streets. The guy has concluded that I can't have gone far on foot, and he must have gotten neighbors to help him look for me. They go up and down the street several times and then I lose sight of them.

I stretch out on my bed and the skeleton on the motorcycle seems to be looking at me and laughing.

A CAR

Sometimes we arrive at work about fifteen minutes before the prior shift goes home, and we usually spend the time in the parking lot, talking. One afternoon when I arrive, George and his brother-in-law, the Vampire, are sitting inside George's car, smoking pot. A few seconds later, a tall, fat twenty-year-old Chicano, Juan, shows up. Then comes Javier, the Little Ox, in his old car. He leans out the widow and greets us in his usual way, "What's happening, dudes. Don't burn it alone, roll your friends a joint." Then he parks his car a couple of spots from us and comes over, obviously in a good mood.

"Hey, dudes, I've bought me a pickup," he says, waiting for us to join in his glee.

"It was about time, you son-of-a-bitch," George says acidly. "I thought you were going to die in that old car and be buried with it. What are you going to do with it now, send it to the junk yard?"

Javier doesn't answer. Instead, he looks back at his old car, as if George had made him recall that he ought to think about what to do with it.

"My little old car," he says to himself as if he'd only now realized that he was replacing it and as if he had to ask its permission.

He walks back to the car and lays a palm atop its roof, which is peeling and rusted in places. He looks at all the dents in it, some deeper than others, and walks around to the back of it, without taking his eyes off of it.

"If this car could talk ... ," he says, looking back towards us. "If it could talk, it would tell you stories, dudes, lots of stories. How many wetbacks we've carried from Laredo to Houston, Dallas or here! Always full of power, dependable, running like nothing. Carrying a load of wetbacks, we've run right alongside highway patrolmen, and they've suspected nothing. Me at the wheel cold with sweat, but they never stopped me."

"That car would be good for you," George tells me. "If you keep on walking everywhere, it's easier for *La Migra* to grab you."

106

"What the dude says is right," Javier tells me, thinking that he can get more money from me than from the junkyard. "I'll sell you my car. It's a little ugly, but it holds up. Two hundred dollars and it's yours."

I don't take what George says about the *Migra* into account. For several months I've been walking to work and back, and going downtown, and I haven't seen one of the green-suited *Migras* since the time when I first tried to cross the border. Sure, I've got the idea of buying a car, but not right away, and besides, Javier's car isn't very attractive. It is hard to imagine what it looked like in its better days. It's a Pontiac, with four doors, a gold-colored exterior, scratched and dented, and a plastic-covered roof, now all peeling away. The trunk doesn't close very well, either. The black seat covers are stained from liquids that have spilled inside, no doubt, mostly beer. In some spots, foam rubber pokes out of holes in the fabric, as if it were trying to get away. A blank space occupies the spot on the dashboard where its radio once sat. You only have to stick your head into a window and you'll smell the stink of age and mold.

"At the most, I'd give you a hundred dollars," I say, hoping that Javier will withdraw his offer to sell.

"Sold to the dude!" he exclaims.

He reaches out to shake my hand, and with his other hand, reaches into his pocket, takes out his keys and gives them to me.

"*No me rajo*," "I not backing down," I tell him.

Then I take out my billfold and give him the hundred dollars.

"You ought to try out the car first," George tells me.

But his advice doesn't make much sense; first of all, because the transaction is already complete. I'm sure that the car runs, because I've seen it come and go out of the parking lot. I don't know anything about cars, not even how to tell if one is running good or badly, and I don't know how to drive. But with help from George and Javier, we make the car go around a few blocks.

When we've finished, Javier tells me that the ownership papers are in the glove compartment, that the motor leaks a little oil—he tells me to add STP to it—and that before taking it out on the street, I should warm it up for at least five minutes, or at least until it stops smoking, so that I won't get a ticket. He also says that the back tires are slick, and that I shouldn't drive fast when it is raining.

Despite the condition of the car, I feel content, just because I own it. I really don't need it. It hasn't been any trouble to walk to work, or to the grocery store, or to go downtown, and the city buses never run late. I think that my feeling of contentment comes from wanting to emulate Americans, and I haven't met one of them who doesn't have a car. Even the sickly Vampire, who earns the same wage that I do, has traded cars a couple of times since I came to work at the printshop. George, our foreman, has one car for workdays and another for taking trips with his family on weekends, just as in Mexico, where I had two changes of clothes, one for weekdays and one for Sunday wear.

The car doesn't let me down, either. It starts without hestitation, the accelearator and brakes work fine, and I don't have to move around in the seat to raise or lower the windows, which are operated by pressing buttons in the driver's door panel. On top of that, the car's heavy steel body makes me feel like I'm driving a tank.

The day before Halloween I receive a letter from my parents, saying that they are fine and that one of our cows has given birth to a beautiful calf. In the letter, they remind me that the Day of the Dead is coming up; they tell me that they understand that I can't be with them, and they wish me the best in celebrating it. I write back a long letter to them, telling them about my job at the printshop, about the novelty parked in front of the house where I live, and about the nostalgia I feel for the All Souls Day and Day of the Dead festivals in our village.

Anybody would miss our celebration. I can almost hear the tolling of the bell from the church tower, while up and down the streets the cross is carried by someone who, because of the gravity the ceremony, appears to be a walking statue. With a missal in his hands the cantor walks alongside, repeating the Our Father, keeping rhythm with his steps. On the other side of the cross goes whoever is responsible for carrying the vase of holy water. He dips a yellow *zempoalxochitl*, or dead mans' flower, into the vase, withdrawing the flower to make the sign of the cross on every door. Behind these three figures follows a crowd of those who like to accompany the cross, many of them children. All of them must be respectful; it is forbidden to laugh or play. To make sure that gravity and order are kept, the *Ta ruehda*, or keeper of the church keys, goes along, supported by his helpers who are armed with the *Yetih shquia*, a type of quirt made from the penis of a bull. It is an effective tool for punishments, but it also gives rise to mischief. Some of the companions of the cross always try to provoke a punishment, by laughing behind the backs of innocents, for example. When that happens, the hand that holds the quirt cuts through the air until it cracks on the shoulders or back of the individual who is suspected, who can accuse someone else if he wants.

One time a friend of mine named Ignacio was infatuated with one of the girls in the village, but he hadn't made his feelings known, even though she was waiting for him to tell her. On the feast of All Saints Day—the day prior to Day of the Dead— Ignacio followed the cross to her house. When it got there, he brought punishment on himself several times, in order to show the girl that he was really *macho*. The next day Ignacio went walking in the streets, his back striped with the bruises the whip had left, and the young woman took that opportunity to offer help in healing his wounds.

After they've prayed for the dead, the householders give the companions of the cross shots of *mescal*, baked sweet potatoes, oranges, chewing gum, whatever they can afford to give. Then the man carrying the cross leads the procession on to the next house. The cantor and carrier both tire, and have to be replaced every few hours, and the companions of the cross tire, too, but new followers join the procession. After all of the houses have been visited, the cross returns to its place in the church until the next year.

In my parents house, the altar is probably completely adorned with *zempoalxochitl* flowers, turkey crest flowers and rat flowers, and with bunches of bananas of all kinds, with oranges, lemons, candies, *mezcal*, tortillas, red *mole*, tamales, cookies, soft drinks, water, chocolate, beer, breads made in the shape of people, and in the middle of it all, a cooked chicken. Everything is arranged around the images of the saints so that at the appointed hour, the dead can come and savor these delicacies, because they won't be served like this again until next year.

During one of these festivals, I remember talking to my short little grandmother. We had asked her how she knew that the dead come back on their day. She said that she'd known of a case of a daughter who had told her dying mother that if she returned from the grave, she wanted her to make a sign. The two had agreed that the sign would be a noise made by shaking their kitchen table. When the mother died, the daughter anxiously awaited All Souls Day to prepare the altar and to wait for her mother's return at midnight. My grandmother said that the daughter saw her mother come into the door, accompanied by other spirits walking single file, each of them with a candle in hand. As they'd agreed, the mother went to the table and shook it. As she and the spirits walked out, each handed a candle to the daughter. When the sun came up the next morning, relatives of the daughter found her dead in the doorway. The candles in her hands had turned into a bundle of bones.

"Why did the daughter die?" we'd asked my grandmother.

"Her mother took her with her, so that the daughter wouldn't continue suffering in this world," was the answer that my grandmother gave.

In our village, the festivals of the dead last two or three days, during which no one works. But here in the United States there's no great celebration, as my parents imagine. I tell them in my letter that people work as usual during what is called Halloween, and that at night, the people dress up like warlocks, or hunchbacks or pirates, or in short, any disguise that seems frightening, so that they can get together with friends, dance and drink beer. That kind of celebration seems simple and cold, to my point of view.

Of course, I also tell them that the children dress in disguises and go from door to door saying "Trick or Treat," which is about like saying, "Candy or I'll harm you," and the owners of houses keep on hand a good store of sweets to give the children. I spend Halloween night with the landlady, giving candy to the children who come by. She tells me that the children have sometimes done damage on Halloween, breaking windows and writing on walls.

She recalls for me Day of the Dead celebrations in Querétaro, where she was born, and from which she and her husband emigrated some forty years ago. Her husband had come to Texas as a *bracero*. When his employer arranged permanent immigration papers for him, he went back to Querétaro to bring her. Since then, she's returned only once, in 1965, when her father died. She still has relatives in Mexico, but everyone has lost touch. "Now," she says, "it won't be long before it will be our turn to rest forever."

"You still seem pretty hale," I say, merely not to confirm what she's predicted.

"Ah, what of it? Our time is coming! My husband could go any day, and me, too. All we've got is the house, and we're thinking about selling it, if we can find someone who will let us live here as renters until the end."

"Have you liked the United States?" I ask her, to change the subject.

"Well, I don't know what to tell you. One gets used to wherever one has to in order to make a living. From what I remember of my village, we were poor. Here, we're not rich but at least we have the house and we've raised our children and that's what God has permitted us to do."

Groups of children come by and the landlady gives each of them a fistful of candy. Most of the children are accompanied by their parents.

"Poor things," the landlady says as she watches some children go off, candy-filled bags in their hands. "Today the parents go with their children for fear that somebody is going to poison them, as has happened on some Halloweens. There are people who are sick in the head who've put poison or pins in the candies, and some children have died because of this. All of a sudden there are crazy people all over the United States," she says.

THE WAITRESS

One Saturday morning, after a long sleep that takes away the exhaustion of the week's work, and an hour long hot bath, I get behind the wheel of my car and go driving around the streets of San Antonio with no end in mind other than passing the weekend in a pleasurable way. It's not long until noon, and I'm hungry, so I stop at the cafe where I usually eat, just two blocks from the house. Before ordering, I drink a couple of beers. Patty, a short waitress with big eyes and long eyelashes, whom I've invited to go out with me innumerable times, but who never accepts, warns me that if I continue drinking, I'm likely to get drunk.

"Why do I have to stay sober if I've got nobody to worry about except me and my old car," I tease.

She just smiles and goes on about her business.

"I've bought me a car," I tell her, though I know that she's seen me come and go in it.

"I didn't know it was yours," she says, not showing much interest.

"It's a little ugly, but it holds us," I say, repeating the words that Javier used. "It's big," I tell her, while she spreads a tablecloth before me. "I bet it looks like a ghost is driving when I'm behind the wheel."

She laughs at my words because she knows where they're headed.

"I'd like for you to ride with me, so that you can fill my car with your beauty and good cheer," I press.

She smiles and says that she's afraid of cars.

"I understand you very well," I say. "Me and my car have our ugliness in common, but I assure you, we both have strong hearts. Maybe someday I'll get another car, but right now, I'm content with the one I have."

"It's not your car," she says, "it's that I have to work and take care of my mother, who is in bad health."

"I sure hope your mother gets well soon," I tell her.

She says thanks.

THE COPS

Not long afterwards, I find myself driving down the streets of a residential neighborhood. The quiet and the absence of litter give the impression that the area is uninhabited. From time to time I meet cars that are perfectly kept and shining. After a while, I notice that a patrol car is following me. In my rearview mirror I see that the patrol car has two occupants, both white men neatly uniformed. Both of them seem to be staring directly at my jalopy, or that's the impression I get, maybe because they look so authoritarian beneath their hats. I make a turn at the next corner, hoping they'll go on their way, but they turn, too, and keep following at the same speed. It's pretty clear that they're following me and that makes me nervous.

I take pains to keep my speed at the limits the signs announce, and at every turn to use my indicators, so as not to give them a pretext for stopping me. My license plates are current, the lights all work, and the smoke from my exhaust pipe isn't too visible right now. I'm sure that they know I'm a wetback, because people see that immediately, as if they were watching through memory eyeglasses, seeing us crossing the Rio Grande; the drops of water never dry on us. They're still behind me after three more blocks, and I'm sure that they're just looking for a way to stop me, just to prove that I don't have a drivers license, or insurance for the car—much less any insurance for myself. As soon as a freeway comes in sight, I head towards it, trying to show as little fear as I can. But I'm sweating. When they see that I'm headed for the entrance ramp, they fall back, and I breathe a sigh of relief. But I feel like a dog whom a bigger dog has driven out of its territory.

The incident makes me think about my situation. It's clear that I've got no legal right to be driving on the streets of their town, but what the heck, I've got the same right to be in the United States!

I press down on the accelerator, as if to affirm my thoughts, but really it's only a way of recuperating my valor after having wavered and sweated while the cops were behind me. I don't know how much time I spent on the freeway, but when I've composed myself and I take note of the highway signs, I see that I'm headed north. I had no intention of leaving San Antonio, but it's early Saturday and I don't have to return to work until Monday morning, so I keep going. For an instant I think of returning to the cafe to insist with Patty, but then I conclude that the effort would do me no good. I put a tape into the player I've bought for the car.

LOW RIDER

The tape contains the fifties music that the Low Riders like. I bought it one day after I'd spent an evening in a bar downtown. The smelly bar had been crowded that night, stuffed with people. All the tables were full and couples filled the little dance floor, where they danced to music from the juke box. Two Chicano couples stepped in and, after spending a minute at the door looking around, one of the guys went to the bar to order beers for himself and his companions. The other guy went to the juke box, put some money into the slot, and began pushing buttons. They were *pachucos*, but they were dressed as if for a party. Pretty soon Spanish songs stopped playing, and some English-language romantic songs began. I went up to the jukebox to look for the number of a song that was playing; it was "Sixteen Candles." The two *pachuco* couples made a spot for themselves on the dance floor. A few minutes later, one of the guys disappeared and his girl leaned back against the wall, holding her can of beer in one hand and moving her head around to the rhythm, as if she wanted to dance.

She was wearing a black silk dress that came down to her calves, and a belt that attracted the eye to her small waist and the beginnings of her hips. The fine features of her face were covered with makeup whose colors I could not make out in the dim light, but which gave her a savage look. Her hair was combed into a crown at her forehead and backward, falling on her shoulders.

I went over to her and stuck out my hand, to invite her, and without saying a word she joined me on the dance floor. On one side of us the other *pachuco* couple was dancing. I watched the *pachuco* guy and tried to imitate his movements. He stuck his hands deep down into his front pockets, and stretched his neck like a walking rooster, then threw his head back, and put his right foot out, advancing by moving only his knee. Then he moved his head and arms like a boxer looking for an opening in his opponent's defense, and made gestures with his lips like an orchestra conductor.

115

"Are you Low Rider, man?" my partner asked me.

"Yep," I told her. She spoke to me in English, and I spoke back in English. From what I could hear over the din, I had pronounced the word correctly.

"All right!" I heard her answer.

Maybe she thought I was a Low-Rider because I was doing a good job of imitating the *pachuco* guy, or maybe it was my plaid shirt, which wasn't tucked in at the waist, or maybe it was my low cut shoes.

"You like blues songs?" she asked, with shining eyes and smiling lips.

I emitted the same English sound that I'd emitted the first time.

"Oldies," I added, because I'd seen the word written on some Low-Rider cars.

"Right!" she said.

The juke box quit playing, she went back to her spot by the wall, and her man came back. Promptly, they left the bar.

DALLAS NIGHT LIFE

A few hours later, I'm outside of Austin. I think about stopping, but stay on the freeway. In the distance I see a white tower with a clock, and conclude that—since I don't see any other tower—it must be the place where a madman shot at people, something the landlady told me about. Since I can't decide to get off the freeway, pretty soon I'm leaving the city, headed for Dallas. I stop a couple of times en route, once to put gas in the car and once to eat chicken at a Colonel Sanders outlet. To be sure, the fried chicken isn't nearly as delicious as chicken soup would be at home, with all the appropriate seasonings. At home, my mother would send us kids to the chickenhouse to grab the chicken she'd elected to slaughter, and the one who caught it was entitled to the breast. The event always occasioned a great battle in the chickenhouse, not only between us, but also between us and some of the roosters, who tried to defend their chickens by pecking at us.

It is dark by the time I get to Dallas. As I go into the downtown I notice that, like San Antonio, its buildings are a mixture of new and old. By chance I wind up beneath a concrete bridge from which I can find no exit in the darkness, but off to the side I see a parking lot where several cars have stopped. I pull my car into file. Without getting out, I look around, and notice what seems to be an old building in the shadows. It has a neon light that says, "Starck Club." Music is resonating from inside. I decide to go in.

At the entrance a tall young man says something to me in English, but the noise is loud and I don't understand what he says. I stop walking, wondering what he wants. He extends ten fingers of his hand, close to my face.

"Ah," I say, "ten dollars?"

"Yeah, *diez dólares*," he says, trying to speak Spanish.

The club inside is a big one. On its sides, curtains hang to the floor, partitioning little rooms furnished with comfortable sofas and little coffee tables. Judging by the pipes that come down from the roof to the walls and disappear into the floor, I'm sure that the

place is the basement of an old building. In the center of the room
is a lower area, reached by little sets of stairs, and apparently used
as a dance floor. Two concrete pillars sit in the middle of it.

I haven't gotten over the steep admission price, but now that
I'm inside, I buy a beer and sit down on one of the sofas to drink it.
I figure that this must be a club for rich people, and I'm sure that
I'm right when I see the first clients come in. They are young men
and women, extravagantly dressed. Some of them have purple,
some of them have green, and some of them have orange hair.
Their hair is purposefully tangled-up, sometimes in a crest like a
rooster. The women wear long blouses of loud colors—orange,
lime and canary yellow—and tight pants, some of them made to
look like tiger skin. This is the punk look, I decide.

Some of the men are dressed normally, in sport coats and short
hair. But some of them can't be easily distinguished from the
women because they, too, wear loud-colored pants and have their
hair messed-up in the same way. From a distance, I look at one
guy's face, and it seems to be painted with cosmetics, just like a
woman's. Because the light is dim and I want to be sure, I walk
up closer and see that it's true, the guy is wearing makeup. I can
only tell that he's a male because his chest is completely flat.

I am also surprised to see that moving among the clients are a
young man and woman who look like wets. The woman is wearing
a red apron, and like the young man, is carrying a dust pan in one
hand and a broom in the other. Each has a towel hanging from
a shoulder. They don't stop walking and looking, searching for
something to sweep up with their brooms. I ask myself if there
can be any place where wetbacks haven't arrived, and decide that
even in the White House wets are probably doing the cleaning.

Within an hour the place has filled with strange-looking people.
There's not a moment of silence, as one record follows another
on the loudspeaker system. People are now on the dance floor
below: ordinary couples, couples of men only, one woman with two
men, and a few people who are dancing alone. More extravagantly
dressed people arrive. Two of them are dressed in leather shorts,
jackets that come only to their midriffs, and matching bracelets.

"*¿Quihubo, paisano?*" "What's happenin', countryman?" I ask
the wet when he passes by, looking for something to sweep.

His accent is Central American and he tells me that he's from
El Salvador.

"What can you tell me about the war in your country?" I ask
him.

"It's been a long time since I left home, but back then, the war didn't let you work in my village. I don't know anything now, only what I see on television, but the war has to be about the same, I guess."

"Whose side were you on when you were in El Salvador?"

"On nobody's side," he answers. "That's why I came to the U.S. Here I can work in peace."

Another wet appears at the entry door. He's short and paunchy. It's easy to see that he's already drunk. Without losing any time, he starts extending his hand to girls, inviting them to dance. He makes a full circle, inviting, but nobody accepts. He looks down on the dance floor, then begins to dance by himself, right where he's standing.

When I go to find the restrooms, I find that they are marked by signs projected from film, as if they were photo slides. The signs aren't in English or Spanish, either. One says "Femme," and the other, "Homme." I don't have any trouble understanding them, however, because the words are close enough to Spanish. While I'm at the urinal, I look around and see a woman leaning up against the wall. I think for a minute that maybe I've taken the wrong door, but then I know I haven't, because women can't use urinals. I'm in her sight, but she doesn't seem to notice me. I look at her face and she seems lost in her thoughts. She may not even know that she's in a restroom, I decide.

On leaving the restroom I pause for a minute at the door, and notice that men are entering at the womens' door. My curiosity leads me to push the womens' door open a crack. I wait for a moment, expecting somebody to tell me that I can't go in, but nobody says anything or looks my way. I go in and behold a half dozen white women, gathered in what appears to be an anteroom, sitting on a sofa similar to those in the main part of the club. Hanging high on one wall is a television showing pictures of a swimming pool. A few other women are standing before mirrors on the walls. I expect gestures of surprise to greet my entrance, but just like the woman I encountered in the other restroom, none of them pays any attention. They continue combing their hair or retouching their makeup as if nothing unusual was happening. I take a seat on one of the sofas and light a cigarette.

One of the young women raises her dress to adjust her panties, showing her white legs and her rear, which shakes with every twist she gives her undergarments. Then she unbuttons her blouse and before my eyes I see her breasts and pink nipples.

"Help me put on the cream," she says to another of the young women, putting a little bottle between her hands.

They say something among themselves, but apparently not to avoid my hearing. The second young woman massages the cream onto the first, and the first woman's bust disappears beneath her blouse again. The first one combs her hair for a minute, and then leaves the restroom.

A little while later the Salvadoran comes in, and I congratulate him for working in such an attractive environment.

"Well, yes, man," he says, "we see spectacles like this every day, but there's no way to warm up these chicks, because they've got only cocaine in their veins. Just look at their stupid faces and you'll know."

"At least you've got something to look at," I tell him. "And I'll bet that at least one of them has fallen for you."

"Ah, what are you talking about!" he protests. "Here, if you want to conquer a woman, you'd better look like one. Or if you've got a little bit of cocaine, any of them will open their legs, my buddy, but you should see what that powder costs. Just a little bit of it," he says, showing me the tip of his little finger, "costs as much as I make in a week."

A blonde of about eighteen, with long, tangled hair, dressed in a green blouse that comes down past her hips and in crimson stockings for pants, strikes me as the type of young woman the Salvadoran was talking about. Facing one of the concrete pillars of the dance floor, she sways slowly, trying to keep a rhythm and babbling something between her lips. Her stare is fixed on the pillar as if she has mistaken it for her dancing partner. After a minute, she throws her arms around it, and then resumes swaying, at first with her cheek still touching the pillar. Little by little she slips downwards until she hits the floor. She lies there, moving her head from side to side, until finally, she rests her head against the pillar, and just sits.

About two hours after coming into the club, I leave, believing that my ten dollars were well-spent, if only because seeing the restrooms was a novelty. I had, in any case, already given up on finding a woman to occupy the place I'd offered Patty. I go back to my car and cruise unfamiliar streets, at times driving all four sides of a block. After a few minutes I come upon an electric sign that says "Topless," and I decide to stop, without giving the matter much thought.

As soon as I pass the main door, my nostrils are assaulted by the smell of something old and humid, like spitoons. Next to the door is a sign saying that a cover charge of two dollars is charged, and I hand my two dollars into a little window like those at movie theatres. The place isn't very big and it's not nearly as extravagant as the Starck Club. The clientele is completely different. The Starck was filled with people who looked as if they'd never worked a day in their lives. This place is filled with dark-skinned men of all three races, some of them wearing work uniforms similar to those that we wear in the print shop in San Antonio. The place is so crowded that I have to crane my neck to find an empty table, and to get to it, I have to ask permission to pass at each of the tables along the way, because people have bunched together, even put their tables together. On one side of the room is a bar, and on the opposite side, a stage, at eye level. It looks like a port town dock, adorned on its edges with blinking colored lights.

Suddenly, a drum roll sounds, as if to tell the audience to be quiet. Then there's the sound of a saxophone, followed by the voice of a singer, as if it, too, were an instrument. The lights on the stage begin to blink to a faster tempo.

"All, right!" people in the audience shout when the drum does a long roll. Then they whistle and shout "Good! Good!" meanwhile applauding. And not without reason. A svelte black woman appears on the stage and slides, more than walks, around its perimeter with practiced movements. She dances so smoothly that at times I find myself wondering if the music isn't coming from her, instead of the band. She raises her thin arms above her head, then drops them onto her shoulders, to peel off her halter, and holding it upon her breasts, she walks to the edge of the stage to offer them to the audience. One of the men stands up to touch her with his mouth, she darts effortlessly back to center stage. She pulls her hands away from her breasts, taking the halter with her, and then casts it to the stage floor, revealing her nude torso. She moves her hands time and again across her nipples, without missing a note of the music, then moves them down to her stomach to unfasten her G- string, which, like the halter, she lets fall to the floor. Her hands play at her hips as she simulates copulation, and then she moves to the edge of the stage and kneels before a customer who, with his mouth open and without taking his view from her, takes out a bill and puts it into a thin elastic band on her waist, her last stitch of clothing. She turns her back to the crowd and bends down until her hands are touching the stage floor, her hips pulsing above. The crowd roars. She makes the rounds of the edges of the stage, and her little elastic belt fills with money. The music stops playing and as it does, with the same agility as in her dance, she collects her minimal clothing from the floor and disappears behind a door.

After this show, the lights around the stage go dark and the place fills with music again. A side door opens and a group of young black women come out into the club, dancing in the little spaces between tables. After observing what the object of this ritual is, I imitate what I've seen. From a distance I pick out a dancer and attract her attention. With my index finger I signal her to come to my table. She comes as if I'd pulled her on a string. Without saying a word, she climbs atop my table and dances, raises one leg and then another, and then falls to her knees. Her gaze goes from my face to the elastic band on her thigh, and from the elastic band to my face. I put a dollar bill into the string and she rises to dance again. She twists and grinds atop the table, and for a moment, I am reminded of the mechanical dancers in music boxes. A moment later she looks at me and at the elastic band again, and I know she's asking for more money. I part with another dollar. As I place it into the band, I feel her skin, soft like velvet and warm. In a friendly but authoritatrian way, she says, "Don't touch!" When she determines that I am not putting more bills into the string, despite her looks from the string to my face, and from my face to the string, she steps down, and without missing a beat, dances over to the table of another lonely guy.

THE WORK WEEK

The coming of Monday signifies that the weekend is over and that we have to begin another week of work, and as with anything, beginning is always difficult. But it helps to know that without Monday, there wouldn't be any Tuesdays, and without Tuesdays, no Wednesdays, etc.—until the work week has passed again. On Mondays, most of my co-workers are tired from their weekend activities, and I imagine the rest of the city is also slumped, because there's never much work for us in the print shop. On Mondays, we produce a few commercial brochures and newspapers of minor circulation, enough to occupy only a few of us, because on most Mondays only two of our eight units are in operation. The rest of us take brooms to do the cleaning, and move rolls of paper here and there. Work is so scarce that we look for trash in even the smallest places, trying to stay busy, because the supervisor is watching. It is not difficult to clean up, but Mondays are tedious because we have to hunt for ways to spend eight hours.

We usually take as much as an hour for lunch on Mondays, without marking it on the time clock, feeling safe in the knowledge that on Mondays the owner doesn't show up. Everybody gathers around the dining table in the lunchroom to talk about what he did over the weekend.

Mario, the ink-keeper, a short man with a dark complexion, is a wrestling fan. He tells us about the matches he saw, or watched on television. He lifts weights on the weekends, with the illusion of someday being a wrestler like those he sees on television. He's young enough to realize his ambition—about twenty years old—but his stature won't help him much. The guys in the shop have derisively named him "El Emascarado," or the "Masked Man," because masked wrestlers are a Mexican motif.

The Ox and his brothers spend weekends playing billiards, and on Mondays they brag about their feats with the cue.

Sometimes, when there's not much news to tell from the weekend, the guys at work fall back on older stories. They also tease me,

123

asking, for example, if we have cars in my village, and for months, they haven't called me by my name. Ever since we printed some magazines that carried an illustration of Geronimo, they've called me Indian Geronimo, saying that I look like him. One of them tore out one of the illustrations and put it on the wall, with my name written below. Just to tease me, every now and then one of them will begin dancing and whooping when I come by, in the manner of Indians they've seen in movies.

My only response has been to tell them that I am a Zapotec from Oaxaca, and to describe for them, with a little exaggeration, the jungle where, I tell them, every hundred yards one encounters deer, bobcats, turkeys, squirrels, eagles and snakes. I also tell them about the the two, crystal clear rivers where, after you've hunted one of these animals, you can build a fire and cook your catch, without needing to buy meats that were frozen days before and have passed through several kitchens before being heated in the shop's microwave oven. They listen with open mouths when I tell them how serious breaches of the law are punished in my village, though in truth, this is something I've never seen and know only because I've heard it from my grandparents. The old folks tell about a gunman who robbed and who burned fields until he was finally caught. They say that they tied him to a tree and cut the skin from his feet, and that after making him walk for several hours, they hung him upside down and cut pieces of flesh from his extremities until only his torso and head were left. Mondays are spent telling such tales.

Hard work begins for us on Tuesdays and grows more hurried every day until Friday, which is so hectic that we begin work the instant we relieve the afternoon shift. Each of us has separate duties. I spend the days moving rolls of paper and taking away the bundles of printed newspapers that are stacked on wooden platforms. Mario, the Masked Man, runs up and down the shop poking his head into presses and craning his neck to make sure that the ink receptacles are always full. The Ox does almost the same thing, making sure that the mixture of water and ink is right. George, standing at the head of the units, controls the folding equipment. Every few seconds he picks up a newspaper and pages through it rapidly, to make sure the imprint is centered and clear. When he notices something wrong, he whistles to Ox and the Masked man, and with hand signals tells them that on such-and-such unit or page, such-and-such correction must be made. When everything is all right, George also presses a button that accelerates the velocity of the presses, which gain speed slowly until reaching their maximum. At that point, the shop fills with such racket that it's impossible to hear anyone talk. The "catchers," Javier and the Vampire, try to keep up with the machines, taking off the newspapers that they so rapidly kick out, and stacking them on wooden platforms. On a run of several thousand copies, it's necessary to stop the presses only to load them with new rolls when they run out of paper. But sometimes, from an excess of water or ink, the paper will tear and a press will stop automatically, with a sound like a drowning man. As soon as that happens, the men whistle and shout accusations at one another.

Every now and then the supervisor, a tall Chicano, leans out the door that goes into the offices. He smiles and claps his hands while shouting to us, "Come on boys, that's the way I like to see you. Get a move on it, just like last night! I want this job done today, not tomorrow!"

The hours pass as quickly as the rhythm the machines keep, and when we're least expecting it, the guys from the next shift show up. It goes that way through Wednesday and Thursday and until Friday, the day when we leave the print shop with our green paychecks.

THE CUBANS

The city is filled with Cubans and I've come to know some of them, because they are good customers of the bars, even better than the wetbacks who regularly attend. One of them is a guy of about eighteen, who says that he's a former university student. He goes from bar to bar, telling the women that he's a poet and reciting verses for them. Once while I am sitting at a bar, two of them come in and order. One of them begins to complain, in a heavy Cuban accent, that he hasn't been able to find work because nobody wants to give a job to an exiled Cuban.

"Well, don't tell them that you're Cuban, chico, tell them that you're Chicano," his companion tells him.

His buddy explodes.

"You're an idiot, chico, you're as stupid as they come! How am I going to tell them that I'm Chicano when I'm Cuban. I may not be in agreement with Fidel, but of being Cuban, I'm very proud!"

One day I notice that at one of the abandoned buildings by the railroad tracks, somebody has removed the sheet of plywood over a window, and I see that a door that was always open has been closed. As it turns out, a couple of Cubans have moved there, and they tell me that the government has given them permission. One of them is a short man in his early twenties, with nappy hair, and the other, who says he's an uncle to the first, is tall, thin, black and about thirty-five. The room that they live in must have been a storage place, because it's huge and they barely occupy a corner of it. Their furniture consists of a pair of cots, an electric hot plate and a few pots and pans. Only one of them works, on a temporary job helping a truck driver load and unload merchandise at a store. The Cuban has invested the money he's made in a .38 calibre revolver and in an old car. His car is so decrepit that it looks shameful beside mine. They tell me that several times they've had to push it home.

The two Cubans are among those who arrived in the Mariel boatlift, they tell me, without going into details. Nor do they tell me anything about their lives back in Cuba. They only say that in Cuba, they didn't have the freedom they have in the U.S. The younger one, they claim, was jailed for merely standing in his doorway in shorts. But after knowing them a few days, I conclude that they are ex-convicts, because in their conversations they frequently make reference to rations and games of chance, and to such-and-such jailer, but never mention anything about having worked.

CHRISTMAS

In December, the streets are decorated with Christmas adornments. On their windows, stores paint pictures of Christmas tree ornaments, of the flowers that in my village we call Saint Catherines, of images of Santa Claus and the words "Merry Christmas." "Have a good day" greetings change to "Merry Christmas." Everywhere it's "Merry Christmas," "Merry Christmas," a greeting that sounds hollow to me, and about the same as "Have a nice day," because it means the same thing: "Thanks for your purchase and we hope you make it back again." But the impression is different at night in the neighborhoods, where through the windows of almost every house I see flashing colored lights on Christmas trees, decorated with glass ornamets, angel hair and greeting cards. Seeing the lights flash on and off in the darkness makes me feel a deep contentment, as when one watches the gentle breathing of a small child in deep sleep. But I also feel melancholy, because I am alone, far from my family and friends.

The pine tree that my older brother planted several years ago at the entrance to my parents house has probably been decorated for the season. I have sent my parents a Christmas card which I imagine has by now arrived. They haven't sent a card to me because that custom doesn't exist in our village. But in every letter they send me greetings that I take more to heart than a mountain of cards printed with identical words.

In our village, storekeepers do not say "Merry Christmas." But everybody celebrates, beginning in the middle of December, when the images of the pilgrim saints are carried out of the church by young people, in hopes that in the coming year the saints will bring them good fortune. Families decorate their houses and family altars with figures cut out of paper, and they make crowns with the leaves of a type of maguey that grows in the mountains. On each end of the altar they put a handful of reeds and beneath the altar, like a carpet, a type of moss that hangs down from trees and that, because of its whitish color, they call "the whiskers of God."

They do all of this so that the traveling images of the saints will have a comfortable stay. The woman of the house, dressed in her best clothing, waits midway between the two houses to be given the image by the woman who kept it the night before. When it is presented, she carries it home in her arms, leading behind her the multitude that includes female cantors, singing praises to the saints, and little boys, popping firecrackers. The young girls run in the middle of the crowd, trying to keep whistling firecrackers from striking them on the feet, though they suffer no harm if the fireworks reach their mark.

These pilgrimages are made every night until Christmas Eve. On that night in the house of the woman who is hosting the image of the baby Jesus, the whole village gathers and is feasted with coffee and slices of bread, until the hour comes when *mole* and chicken are served. At that moment, everybody eats as best he can, because there are never enough tables for the crowd. Some people sit on their haunches with their plates on their knees, others stand here and there in their serapes, warming themselves around the fires that are built on the patio.

During the season, the village also fills with the people who have gone off to live in Oaxaca City, Mexico City and other parts of Mexico. Others come from Los Angeles, just to spend the holidays. We also see new faces, of people not born in the village, the children of parents who long ago left to seek adventure in the cities. Some of the diasporans have done well, while others are still living in impoverished squatter towns, often without water, and without space for their children to play. A few are without work.

I can still remember when, twenty years ago, the village was full of inhabitants. That was back before people began to emigrate to other places. In the afternoons the center of town was crowded with little boys, looking for ways to spend their time, and with teenage boys, gathered in small groups, trying to court the girls who, with the permission of their parents, had also come out to spend the afternoon, or had been sent to buy something at a store. A lot of the young people joined an organization that did agricultural work under the supervision of their elders. At the end of every harvest, the group had a great quantity of corn that they could sell to the families whose harvest had fallen short. After the harvests and the shelling of the corn, there were dances where no admittance was charged, because the dances were organized by the youth society, which paid the musicians in corn. But in the days since then, city life has claimed the young people.

The young people began to emigrate, the young women working as maids in the homes of the rich people, the young men finding work in lots of different settings. At first, they only left for short spells, returning home on their vacations or at festival times, dressed in flashy clothing that was such a novelty that it always caused talk in the village. One of the young women came back dressed in the Mexico City vogue of the time—a miniskirt—and was immediately named, "Miss Cover-Up." Another young lady, whose father went on horseback to meet her at the bus stop, changed clothes when she arrived, into a cowgirl outfit. She came into town on the horse, which her father led by its reins; the people nicknamed her "Juana Gallo," like a character in a western movie.

The young people who went to the cities for only short periods finally married in the cities and settled there. But that was only the beginning, because the desire to study lured others to the cities, especially those who already had relatives living in them. Then, after the secondary school was established in the village, everybody who graduated went to the cities to pursue a career.

Today, the old and the very young inhabit the village, because most of the young adults are wetbacks in the United States or, especially among those who have acquired a career, they have jobs in Mexico, but outside the region. There are not enough people now to fill the streets with noise, the stores close early, and at night, it's as quiet as a desert. At night, every now and then you'll see somebody pass beneath one of the electric lights, and you can hear their footsteps on the gravel long after the darkness has swallowed them. Sometimes the loudspeakers that point towards different neighborhoods from city hall fill the silence with music.

But at festival times an avalanche of people come, hundreds of them, and during these days, the streets are full, the *cantinas* are full, the stores are full, and at dances there's hardly room to move. Groups of young people go up and down the streets, some singing, others chatting, and always someone starts a fight and has to spend the night in jail. Others go from house to house, visiting uncles and godfathers and grandparents, and being served at least a cup of coffee in each one. There is noise, there are people. It is the population of the village, with branches that have grown out and dropped seeds elsewhere. But as soon as the festivals are over, one by one, they all leave, and the village is as before, or worse. Like a creek that widens its canal to become a river, then shrinks to become a creek again, the village seems smaller.

THE JOB APPLICATION

By the time I've been at the print shop a year, I've learned the jobs of the catchers and ink keeper. I've also learned to put photographic plates onto the rollers of our presses, and to center impressions. But beyond that, I haven't learned anything. The management has raised my salary by twenty-five cents an hour—I now make that much above minimum wage—and the laundry has lost two sets of the pants from the six work uniforms that I was issued.

One day while passing through the south side of the city, I see a carpentry workshop and decide to ask for work. I have no need to change jobs, but I think of the use I could make of new skills in our workshop back in the village.

When I go into the office, a young Chicano woman is sitting behind a desk, typing. I ask if they need a carpenter and she says that they don't, but that I should leave my name and telephone number with her, so that the company can call should a vacancy occur. I recite the telephone number of my landlords. She writes it down on a slip of paper and casually sticks it among others papers on her desk.

Before leaving the office, I look at the adornments on its walls, one of which is covered with photographs of the furniture the company makes. Tables, chairs, doors, windows, beds, stairways, all finely finished. Hanging from the ceiling by a pair of light metal chains is a manual plane, cut out of cedar, and at its base, in perfectly cut wooden letters, the name of the company. On seeing it, I ask myself when I will quit seeing things like that in the United States. The plane that has become antiquated here is exactly the same as the one we have in the workshop at home, only ours is for use, not for adornment. I ask myself if I might also seem antique to them, like the plane. Through the doorway that leads into the workshop, I hear noise from electric machines. In the United States, carpentry is carried out amidst thunderous scandal, while in my village, it is carried out in a silence interrupted only by

131

the saw—which produces what to my ears is a gentle melody—the whistling plane, and the dry blow of the hammer on nailheads, sounds all made to the rhythm of our arms.

I say thanks to the secretary for her attention, but she is busy with her adding machine and doesn't hear me. I go out of the office thinking about the difference between home and here, and I feel smaller. It's not that the same type of machines don't exist in Mexico, but there they have import prices, and we can't afford them.

A YULETIDE TRYST

On December 24, we work a normal day in the print shop, but before our shift ends, the owner gives each of us a bonus check. The checks vary according to our length of employment. Mine is for thirty dollars. My co-workers have given me their addresses, saying that if I'd like, I should spend the evening with them and their families. I tell them thanks, but I've already decided not to visit any of them. They will be eating turkey and drinking beer, they've told me. They may think that I'm not grateful for their invitations, but what I foresee at their homes is not really a *fiesta*, but a family reunion, with a family meal like on other festive days in the United States. I decide that I'd rather spend the time in nostalgia for the *fiestas* in my village than spend the evening here intruding upon a family that is not mine.

Before going to the cafe where I usually eat, a idea is dancing in my mind. I imagine that Patty will invite me to have dinner with her and her mother, who she continues to describe as being in bad health. But it's only an illusion. She hasn't accepted any invitations of mine, and more than at any other time, on Christmas she will want to be with her mother. When I get to the cafe, I am served by the cook, a woman of about thirty-five from the state of Michoacán; she is an illegal alien, like me. I am surprised not to see Patty and I ask the cook about her.

"Forget about Patty, young man," she tells me. "She's looking for a better match. She wants to become a citizen."

"Well, where is she?" I persist.

"She has gone on vacation."

We don't say anything more about the subject. She serves me a couple of extra beers and piece of cake, on the house in honor of the season, she says. When I pay and say goodbye, she says "Merry Christmas," just like in other businesses, only she says it in Spanish, *"Feliz Navidad."*

"That's what I hope for," I tell her.

In the street I repeat the phrase, "She wants to be a citizen."

If that's true, I can't be the man. He will have to be a Chicano or
a *gringo*. "She wants to be a citizen," I keep repeating. "Then let
her be a citizen!" I say, almost shouting, barely noticing that other
pedestrians have heard me and are looking at me strangely.

Later on, I get into my old car and head downtown to spend
Christmas Eve, just as at home. I would go downtown to the ash
tree, to sit on the multiform roots which rise above the ground. My
friends would be seated there, each one with a bottle of *mescal*, because a little later on, they'd go to the houses of their girlfriends,
or the houses of those young women they'd like to have as girlfriends, to serenade them. My older brother would play on his
guitar, though not skillfully, but it wouldn't matter much, because
the singers wouldn't be able to carry a tune very well, and besides,
with the household dogs barking, the result would only be a perfect
cacophony. The girlfriend would say that they sing well, because
what counts for her is not the expertise of the serenaders, but their
intentions and their presence.

The bar I frequent downtown is more crowded than usual, and
this means that I'm not the only one who doesn't have a family or
home for spending the night. The Chicano who is standing guard
tonight is as tall and wide as the door, and he has to almost get
on his knees to search me, because I'm only five feet, five inches
tall. After I go inside, I watch him for a few minutes. He stands
at the door, legs spread out, with his arms crossed over his chest.
Only his eyes shine inside his big head, like the marble eyes on rag
dolls. He is a statue of authority, but with his nightstick, pistol and
handcuffs hanging from his belt, I think he overdoes the image.

The juke box isn't still for even a moment. Some men and
women are wearing cone-shaped paper hats of brilliant colors, a
few have masks, and some are blowing on noisemakers. Alcohol
in certain doses can produce great gifts. It makes shyness disappear and unties the vocabulary. A white girl comes into the bar,
seemingly disoriented and repeating in Spanish only the words,
"My Love. That's all. The whole world." She dances to *cumbias*,
boleros, *rancheras* and anything else that might be playing on the
juke box. She is short, thin, with short, ash-blonde hair that looks
mistreated. I never learn how she happened into this bar full of
dark-skinned people, and if she tells me I still don't learn, because
apart from those three phrases, "My love. That's all. The whole
world," she speaks only English. During the hour after she enters,
several men take her onto the dance floor, but a little later, I see
her alone and I go up to her to invite her to a beer and a dance.
She sits at my table talking and talking in English, and I pretend to

understand her. She apparently believes that I understand, because she doesn't quit talking. When she gestures, I gesture. When she laughs, I laugh. When she gives a surprised look, I do the same. And from time to time I say, "Yes."

"Merry Christmas," I tell her when midnight comes.

"That's all," she says.

The night goes on until dawn, when we get into my old car and we head towards my room. She keeps talking, even through her elbows.

"*Es todo*," "That's all," I respond to her from time to time.

The next morning I take her to breakfast. She is still in high spirits when she tells me goodbye, talking so much that she has to move her fork to the side of her lips while she finishes a phrase. But it is enough for me that with her presence she has filled the lonliness of my room and warmed by bed. I tell her goodbye and wish her good luck, but she doesn't understand me. She has asked nothing from me, but without her noticing, I have put a twenty dollar bill in the pocket of her jeans.

"Goodbye love of the whole world," are the last words I say.

"That's all," she says. Then she recites about ten goodbyes for me. She kisses me on the cheek; I feel as if a string is being undone.

THE CARPENTRY SHOP

My old car has begun to fail me. I've had to buy a new battery for it, and every time I check, it needs more oil than before. A mechanic tells me that the generator is no longer working, and I have to go to a junkyard to find another. A few weeks afterwards, when he tells me that the racket it has begun to make means that it needs a new motor, I decide to give up the car. I drive it to the junkyard, where I sell it for thirty dollars.

On a Wednesday afternoon two weeks later, I come home from work and the landlady comes to the door of my room to tell me that a carpentry shop has called, saying that I should come in for an interview.

"The carpentry workshop," I say, trying to recall the place. The shop with the plane finally comes to mind.

This means that more jobs are offered to me than I need, and for the first time since coming to the United States, I feel important. It's quite a contrast from the way I felt when I was going door-to-door saying, "Excuse me, sir, I am looking for a job." Now I imagine that at the carpentry shop the boss will say, "We need you, sir," and that sounds a lot better. The thing is, life makes turns and you never know whether it's going to go straight ahead or backwards.

After thinking about it for several hours, I decide to go to the interview. When I arrive, the same secretary receives me. After making me wait a few minutes, she introduces me to the owner of the shop. He is a Mexican-American about thirty-five years old, short and with auburn hair, dressed in kakhi pants and a cream-colored t-shirt upon whose frontside is printed the figure of the plane that is hanging in the office as a decoration. The same design is on the back of the shirt, except that the backside also carries the name of the company.

"This is the young man that I was telling you about," the secretary says to him.

He looks at me from head to toe, as if he is measuring my

136

capacity.

"Is it true that you are a carpenter?" he asks.

"Sure I'm a carpenter," I tell him.

Then I tell him that I've never made furniture like in the pictures on the walls, which are more complicated than those we make in my father's shop with only manual tools.

"We cut wood from logs with a handsaw, and with a plane like the one on your shirt," I tell him. "We drive nails with an ordinary hammer and make holes with a brace and bit. As far as quality goes, our shop is in a village where there's not as much demand for quality, so long as our furniture is strong and heavy."

"Your experience is valuable," he says, "though here we work with electric tools. With a little practice, you'll be able to handle them."

I also tell him that I have a job in the print shop and that before going to work for him I'd have to quit.

"Very well," he says. "Let my secretary get some information from you and when you're ready to go to work, I'll be waiting in the shop."

The secretary doesn't hand me the job application. Instead, she asks me questions as she completes it. I tell her that I've got four dependents, because the guys at the print shop have told me that if you inflate the number, the government deducts less taxes from your pay. The savings may not amount to much, but I understand that we wetbacks can't get tax refund checks at the end of the year, like citizens can.

When the secretary has completed the form she tells me that my salary will be $3.35 an hour.

Thursday I go to work at the print shop and at the first opportunity, I tell the supervisor that this will be the last week I will work there.

"Where did you learn to quit that way?" he says, a little irritated. "Don't you know that when somebody wants to quit he has to tell the company fifteen days in advance so that it can fill the vacancy? And also because, if you should want to come back here, you'll be accepted?"

"Well, this came up and I didn't plan to leave until yesterday," I tell him.

"Well, if you've already made up your mind, we won't try to keep you," he says.

The following Monday, I present myself at the carpentry shop at 7:30 in the morning. Once I see the workshop I understand why they have relegated the hand plane to decorative purposes.

The shop is about fifteen yards wide and thirty yards long, with concrete walls and a sheet metal roof. It has two circular saws, a bench drill, two band saws, a big sanding machine, six feet tall and five feet wide, two lathes, two angle-cutting saws and four big work tables upon which various power tools like planes, sanders and drills, are laid. Huge stacks of pine, ash, oak, poplar and cedar stand at corners of the building, and more lumber is on shelves of steel tubing that occupy the length of the two longer walls.

As at the print shop, my first tools are the broom and dustpan. I carry mountains of sawdust out of the shop. About an hour after I begin sweeping, eight Hispanic workers come in one after another, the master carpenters. Each one takes his place at work after putting his lunch pail in a corner near his workbench. In a little while, the machines start whining and creaking according to the hardness of the piece of wood they're working upon. The wood starts flying about in the form of sawdust, completely covering the workers, who furrow their brows, trying to keep the fine sawdust from entering their eyes. There's not a minute of silence. When one machine isn't running, another one is.

I spend my days working with sawdust and shelving the pieces of wood that are still big enough to be of some use, and that are scattered everywhere, as if they were reserved for me. The shop doesn't have a timeclock; the secretary keeps the time. The eight masters don't show up at the hour appointed for everyone else. They come in a half hour or more later. When I ask about their tardiness, I'm told that they are paid by contract, not by the hour. Their pay is calculated as a percentage of the value of the items they produce, and I'm told that they earn from two hundred to four hundred a week.

After a few days, I am put to sanding pieces of furnitue that have been finished, and on some days, clients come in with windows, doors or pieces of furniture to have repaired, and the repair work is given to me.

One day, the owner tells me to cut some wood according to measurements that he has written on a slip of paper, and when he sees that I don't have a measuring tape, he sends me to the office for one. In the office, I ask the secretary for a tape.

"I'm going to sell it to you," she says.

I explain that I don't need it to do a project of my own, but for a task the owner has given me.

"That's exactly why I am going to sell it to you," she says.

"Well, fine. In that case, sell me ten of them," I say, thinking that she's teasing me.

"Which do you want, the twelve or sixteen foot kind?" she says.

I take the twelve foot tape.

"That is ten dollars," she quickly tells me.

When she sticks out her hand, palm upwards, I see that she is serious. I've got that much money in my pockets, but I tell her that I don't.

"That's no problem. We'll deduct it from your paycheck," she says.

On payday, my check is ten dollars short.

A few days later when I come into the shop, the owner hands me a t-shirt like the others wear.

"And how much is this going to cost me?" I ask.

"Nothing, it's the company uniform," he says.

It's the first time that I've worked for a company that sometimes gives and sometimes takes away.

DON PANCHO

One of the master carpenters is from the state of Oaxaca, I learn while cleaning the area where he works. His name is Francisco, but everyone calls him *Don* Pancho. He's about sixty years old, a little taller than me, but still short by American standards, with a little bit of a paunch, the result of daily beer drinking. He has a long, gray moustache that makes him appear older than his years, and he walks a slowly because arthritis has affected his legs and is threatening the fingers of his hands. To celebrate our discovery as *paisanos*, we decide to drink a few beers on the parking lot after work.

Don Pancho has been in the United States since 1964, and he'd been a carpenter before that, too. His experience in the trade is pretty thorough.

"It's been two years now that I've been ready to leave the United States for good," he tells me, "and I don't know why the devil I haven't done it. In every letter I get from my family they tell me to come back to them."

Then he lays his own puzzlement to rest. "Maybe it's because I'm hoping to reach retirement age and collect a pension. I'd like to retire and go to Mexico, to stay. That's what I'll do, if illness doesn't make me retire sooner."

"So, you're legally in the country," I say, figuring that he must be legal if he plans to collect Social Security. No wetback can collect Social Security, even though, as in my case, they take it out of our paychecks.

"No, I'm not legalized, but my Social Security number, the government did give me that. It's legal. You see, before it was easy," Don Pancho says. "All I did was write, asking for a number, and the Social Security card came by mail."

I tell him that the number I'm using is false.

"Things have changed," he says. "I don't know why but before it was easier. And you're not the only one who has used a false number, almost everybody does in order to have something to write

140

on the employment application. The bad thing is that since you're not registered, you can't claim part of the income taxes that the government gives back to you. When you're not registered, the government hangs onto your taxes and a whole lot of other things."

"I put down that I've got four dependents," I tell him.

"That's good, that's a good way to do it," he says, laughing. "You come in illegal, and you have to keep living illegal. There's no other way. Before, it was easier."

Don Pancho raises a can of beer to his lips and doesn't lower it until it is empty. Then he crushes it in his fist and tosses it in a corner next to the workshop's trash barrels.

"For example," he says after burping, "right now, with much pleasure I'd take the first plane to Mexico. But in a few hours, I'll decide to stay here. I think that's probably what people call ambition for money. I'm sick, and I can barely walk. In the mornings, I have to get up an hour earlier than I used to, just to start exercising my legs, so that when the time comes for me to go to the shop, I'll be able to move them. What could it be?" he asks himself, and he looks at me, as if asking me the same question. "Is it love of money or is it that I love to work?"

"I'd say it was necessity," I answer.

"Necessity? I don't need to work anymore. The money I've made while working here I've invested in Oaxaca. I've got several million pesos in the Bank of Oaxaca, and my account pays me monthly interests that I could spend to live tranquilly, without any worries. For years my wife has been running an apartment house and the money for the rents just falls on her every month. Then too, there's the fruit juice bar that we've got downtown. My four children are grown. One of them has graduated in some kind of engineering, I don't know what kind, but he's an engineer. The other is a doctor. My daughter is a teacher and the fourth one is about to finish his university studies. How do you see it? I don't need to work!"

"We were poor when we lived in Oaxaca," he continues. "I worked as a carpenter in a miserable shop, and I earned a miserable salary, and my wife had to sell her fruit juices on a little wooden table in front of our house, that was how she helped us get by. Now, I think that's it's just for pride that she sells fruit juices made with modern machines in a modern setting."

"But just any one of these days, *paisano*, I'm going. You'll see," he adds.

"How many years will it be until you are sixty?" I ask him.

"A year and a half."

"Well, maybe then we'll see each other in Oaxaca, and we can drink a few beers to your retirement," I tell him.

"Of course we will!" he says.

THE BOSS' PET

After Don Pancho and I have become friends, I go to him every time I have difficulties with tasks the others order me to do. He always shows me a way out of my problems, with the patience that only age can confer. Because of his physical condition, he is assigned only those jobs that require more skill than agility or strength, like engravings in wood or other fine finishing work.

Once, while I am cutting a piece of wood on a circular saw, I carelessly let the measuring tape get into the saw blades. About ten inches of the tape fly off into the air and fall into the sawdust accumulated on the floor. I need the tape to keep working on the job, and I see that it will be necessary to go to the secretary to get another one.

"Do you want one just like the other?" she asks me.

I tell her that I do. She reaches under her desk and hands me another tape, and as soon as she's done that, she demands that I pay her ten dollars for it.

"But it was an accident. It happened while I was working for the shop," I tell her.

"It doesn't matter," she says with indifference. "The tape costs ten dollars."

"Well, then I'll do without one, because the most reasonable thing is that I'd give you the one that's damaged, and you'd give me a new one," I tell her.

"No, it's not like that," she says. "Those are the owner's orders."

"Then I'll do without a tape," I say.

That same day, on leaving the shop, I go to a hardware store where I buy a tape that is twenty-four feet long. It costs me only four dollars and fifty cents.

A measuring tape isn't a big item for me to buy for myself, but it's a clear sign that in the shop, things aren't all as they're supposed to be. On the other hand, I am learning to build furniture. The owner has figured a way to take advantage of the experience of

143

Don Pancho, by giving us a list of furniture to build. I take charge of carting the sticks of lumber and of cutting them on the saws, and Don Pancho supervises me step by step. Under his direction, we've finished several pieces which haven't disillusioned the boss, and now I'm spending more time building furniture than cleaning the shop.

One morning, the owner comes in with another wetback who he claims to have recruited in a nearby park called San Pedro. He says that he only asked if the wet, whose name is Roberto, was looking for work, and of course, Roberto wasn't waiting for anything else. Roberto is from Monterrey, and according to what he says, he came to the United States to earn money for continuing his studies in mechanical engineering. He says he only needs two more years to graduate. At first, just like me, he is merely the boss of the dustpan and broom, but before long, he has an opportunity to demonstrate his mechanical skills. When a motor of a circular saw stops running, Roberto volunteers to find the reason why, and before the day is over, the motor is shrieking as always. The owner is happy to have a technician among his employees, at minimum wage, and Roberto is returned to the dustpan and broom with a little extra status.

One afternoon, Robert makes conversation, as any new worker would, to learn what goes on in the shop.

"Well, things here are fine," I advise him. "But if I were you, I'd keep track of my own hours, or else the secretary can discount them, as happened to me. Now I carry a little notebook to keep track of the time I come in, how long I take for lunch, and the hour I leave." I also tell him that it would be best if he'd buy a measuring tape at a hardware store.

One morning, a little after we've begun to work, Arturo, another one of the workers, is injured while working at the circular saw. The saw cuts off the tip of his index finger. Blood spurts out all over his forearm while he watches it with eyes opened wide with shock, fear and pain. "My finger!" he shouts, looking all around as if for help. One of the workers runs into the office and comes back in a flash, carrying gauze, cotton and alcohol. When his hand has been bandaged, Arturo leaves the shop.

The following day, he doesn't show up, and the owner tells me that I should finish the work that Arturo had begun.

"Arturo cut himself on purpose," the boss says, while showing me what is to be done. "He cut himself so that he could have a few days off and collect his salary meanwhile."

"That's the way Mexicans are," he continues. "That's the way that kid has always been."

The owner takes a piece of wood and goes up to the saw to show me how to place my hands while sawing.

"The left hand should always be placed forward when you're sawing. So how is it that he cut his right finger? It was intentional!" he says.

I hadn't seen how Arturo had hurt himself, but I ask myself if anybody is capable of cutting off part of a finger just to get a few days off from work with pay. Just because it was his right, and not his left index finger, doesn't seem to me sufficient proof that the injury was intentional, because both hands are working on the machine, and accidents do happen.

When Arturo comes in later that day with a doctor's prescription in his hands, I understand what the boss had planned. Arturo comes in looking worried and irritated at the same time. He directs himself towards one of the guys who is on his way to his post at work.

"Are you the one who told the boss that I cut myself on purpose?"

The boss had told him that one of the workers had seen him cut himself on purpose.

"The owner invented that story so that he wouldn't have to pay you for your time off," I tell Arturo. Then I notice that behind me stands Roberto, who has become the boss's favorite worker.

"Who told that to the owner?" I then ask Roberto, hoping to make him confess in some way. But he says that he doesn't know, and he looks away, evasively.

Apparently, the owner's plan doesn't work. Arturo collects his pay on the days when he's off.

But from then on, the boss misses no opportunity to hassle me. Me and Don Pancho are producing furniture as rapidly as ever, but he always demands that we work with more speed. I suspect that Roberto has told him what I said to Arturo. Roberto may have also told him what I said about the secretary and the measuring tapes.

One day, I cut some boards to a bad measurement, and that is sufficient cause for the boss to express his dissatisfaction with me.

"Lately you've been slow, and if on top of that, you are now going to have to do your work two times, that's not in my interest. I thought that you were a master carpenter, but now I see that you don't know anything," he says.

After work, I comment on the matter to Don Pancho and tell him that I think it would be better if I quit.

"You can quit if you want, but if I were in your shoes, I wouldn't do it," he says. "Here, more than anything else, you can learn the trade, and that will be useful to you when you return to your village. On top of that, when one comes to this country, he comes to be exploited and humiliated. We want to make money and save it to go back, and we have to realize that it isn't easy. We've got to put up with mistreatment."

I follow his advice, but only for a few more weeks, until I am myself satisfied with my work. The owner isn't there when I decide to announce that I'm quitting, so I tell the secretary instead. Once I get home—it was a payday—I look at my check and notice that I've been given a raise of twenty-five cents an hour. Buoyed by the raise, I spend the weekend thinking that I should go back to the shop on Monday, but when seven o'clock comes on Monday morning, I am still stretched out in my bed, feeling proud that I have succeeded in impressing the boss with my work.

HEAVY METAL

It has been about eight days since I quit the carpentry job. I've been going from one side of town to another without hitting on anything, but without the worries that I had eighteen months earlier when I arrived in the United States. Now things are different. I have repaid the money I owed to my friend in Houston. I have a few hundred dollars saved, including two checks from the carpentry shop that I haven't cashed. On top of that, I've bought a pretty good radio/cassette player.

I've spent my time going to the movies, and I also happened by a music concert. I was walking by the Hemisfair Tower one Saturday afternoon when, next to the Convention Center, I see a group of mostly young people formed in line beside a ticket window with bars on its window. Since I don't have anything to do, I fall in line. Somebody tells me that the line is for a concert of "heavy metal" music, but of course, I'm not sure what that might be. Entry costs me eight dollars.

The inside of the auditorium is shaped like a mechanical thread, in whose center stands a circular stage, surrounded by ascending rows of seats and stairs. The place is filled with young people, mostly Chicanos, dressed in black t-shirts with different designs on their front and back sides. Some of them wear bandannas on their heads, and others have them wrapped around their wrists.

Pretty soon the lights are turned out and wild cheering starts and, one by one, some pink lights come on, which give the impression that we are in the firmament, surrounded by stars. Then an almost complete silence comes over the crowd; only the sound of a thousand breathing throats can be heard. But this is only for a few seconds, because almost immediately the deafening peel of a bell begins, so loud that its sound waves must have reached the border. The noise leaves my eardrums ringing in echo. No sooner has the first round quit than another and another break out. The people seated around me are euphoric, like everybody in the auditorium. A spotlight comes on and is directed onto the stage, forming a

147

small circle. Some shrieks from an electric guitar ring out at the same time that a guitarist, who seems more like a puppet, runs out taking big and small steps, bowing to the front and back, and throwing himself to the ground to rebound like a spring, without ever missing a note on his instrument. Some more lights come on, revealing the rest of the musicians, who have been hidden in the darkness. The scandal lasts only a few minutes, but the music continues. The spectators, most of whom have been on their feet, take their seats and begin moving their heads in rhythm.

The smell of marijuana smoke begins drifting through the rows of seats. A joint passes from hand to hand until it becomes nothing more than a glowing ember. People smoke it as it passes, seeming to inflate and shrink themselves as they do. When the joint comes to the guy on my right he puts it to his mouth, and after taking a long, deep drag, he offers it to me. When he sees that I don't reach out for it, he tells me in a forced voice—so as not to lose the smoke from his lungs—"*Llégale a la mota*, brother!" I puff on it as he did, and when I offer to return it, he tells me to pass it along to the person on my left. A little later, another joint comes along, this time from my left, and another, and another passes, filling the air with piquant smoke. My eyelids begin to feel swollen, my head gets bigger than normal, and my mouth feels so dry that I have to go to the snack bar to buy something to drink.

The music continues and in front of the stage the spectators raise clinched fists in the air, in a way that I had only seen at political demonstrations in Oaxaca City, except there, no marijuana had been in evidence. A few couples dance in the aisles, and here and there, groups of young people chat in shouts, so that they can be heard over the music. Others sit as still as their chairs, and some walk around their seats, moving their heads in time. The most euphoric gather near the stage, which is filled with smoke; the musicians seem to be swimming in clouds of it. I can't make out the rhythms; it all seems like confusing, unrelated sounds to me. After about an hour it all sounds monotonous to me. I am no longer hearing anything that sounds new, and I decide that it's best to leave the auditorium.

SAYING GOODBYE

One day, upon reviewing the pile of letters that I've received from my parents, I note that in one of them they have sent me the address of relatives who live in California. I immediately try to call my relatives from a public phone, but when I can't understand the operator, because she speaks only English, I go back to my room where the landlady helps me place a call from her telephone. I am able to talk with my uncle Vicente, who seems pleased to hear from me. My father had already told him by letter that I was in the United States, without saying where. I ask if there is room for me for a while in my uncle's place, and he says that it's a big house, and I'm welcome anytime. I begin to think about the trip.

I keep going to the same cafe as always, but now with less interest, because Patty doesn't show up anymore. The cook tells me that she has gotten a job at a high-class place, made possible because now Patty speaks a little English. I ask the cook for the name or address of the restaurant where Patty is working, but she refuses to give it to me, saying that I'd best set my eyes on someone else.

"Ah, the citizenship thing," I say, as much to myself as to the cook.

"She'll manage to get it, because she's pretty," I add.

"We'll see," she says.

"No, you will see, because I'm leaving San Antonio," I tell her.

"And for where?"

"Maybe to California."

"They say that it's pretty there."

"Well, I'll tell you if I'm ever back in these parts," I say.

"I wish you good luck," she says.

"Thanks, because I'm going to need it," I tell her.

My landlady helps me reserve a plane ticket, which costs only one hundred dollars for the trip from San Antonio to Los Angeles. I pack my few belongings, which still fit inside a single suitcase.

From L.A. to Oregon

THE UNCLE'S PLACE

My uncle and three other townsmen live in a garage apartment that belongs to an Arab family in the neighborhood of Alhambra. Although my arrival brings the number of us living in the apartment to five, there is sufficient space. Everybody from the village lives in the same way. We rent big apartments so that four to ten people can live in them, and so as to save money on rent and be able to save money for our returns. It is also so that we can be in a position to help other arriving townsmen. My uncle's apartment— the rental contract is in his name—is a wooden building with sheetrock interior walls and two rooms. One is the kitchen, about fifteen by fifteen feet in size, equipped with a stove, sink, refrigerator and, in the middle of the floor, a pretty dining table finished in cedar. The apartment also has a washer and dryer. The kitchen's only adornment is an electric clock, designed in the shape of a coffee pot, that produces a noise as if it were cooking. Lights in its upper part simulate the effect of steam bubbling or streaming out of it.

To one side of the kitchen is the bathroom. To the other is the bedroom, about fifteen by fifty feet in size. It is furnished with a couple of beds with mattresses and some cots, and along one walls stands a varnished pine cabinet. Hanging on one wall, over the headboard of my uncle's bed, is a small frame with a picture of his family. His wife sits in the middle of three children, holding the fourth in her arms. My uncle is forty-three years old, and for fifteen years he's been working in the United States, coming home only to visit his family. He's a mechanic. He's been practicing that trade since his youth, when he worked on big farms and ranches in the tropical part of Oaxaca. He was a tractor driver at first, but little by little, purely by practice, he became a mechanic on farm machinery, even though he had only a fifth grade education in the village. Now he works for a good wage in a Toyota agency. He always wears a work uniform, brown pants and a cream-colored shirt. Besides being a mechanic, he's also a body shop man, a painter, a welder, and on top of all that, a gun repairman, a trade that keeps him busy when he makes his trips home.

He asks me if I've been going to English classes; he seems to be very disappointed when I tell him that I haven't.

"Well, if you want to advance in the United States, you've got to learn English," he says. "If you don't, you'll have to resign yourself to little jobs like dish washing, just like a lot of our townsmen."

Antonio, nearly forty years old, one of the roommates of the garage apartment, is a dishwasher. Rubén, twenty-two, was a dishwasher until recently, but he is now a cook's assistant in the same restaurant where Antonio works. The other roommate is Benjamín, who works as a helper in a body shop and who owns a car that is plenty similar to the one I had in San Antonio, except that it's white.

THE CAR WASH

On the Saturday after I arrive, my uncle takes me to look for work. He takes me directly to a car wash four blocks from our house, where I am immediately accepted. As soon as I've filled out the application, I am given a white plastic bottle with a sprayer and a set of white overalls, a little too big for me. Everybody at the car wash is a wetback, except maybe the foreman, who, with great luck, might be a legal resident. I am put to work under the supervision of a short, fat wetback with an angular face and wide sideburns.

"Hey, Simeón," the manager calls to him. The manager is a tall man with long legs who works a little bent over, as if his head weighed heavily upon him. "Simeón, I'm turning over this *paisano* to you. "*Trinéalo en el jale*," he says, a Chicanismo that I took to mean, roughly, "Train him for the job."

In Mexico, I never would have imagined that it could be necessary to build great machines and put together a team of at least fifteen men, just to wash cars. The job always seemed to me one that you'd do in your spare time, as when a client wanted his car washed when I worked on a parking lot in Mexico City. There, I'd wash them in off-minutes, with a bucket and a rag. On Sunday afternoons in Mexico City, I also noticed men washing their own cars, or having their children or servants do the job, with hoses in hand, at curbside by their homes. I hadn't imagined that washing cars could become a big, specialized business.

The clients come in and drive their cars up to a place where two wets are waiting, with the hoses to vacuum cleaners in their hands. Quickly, they clean the floors and rugs, one working on each side of the car. A driver comes along and takes the car onto some rails and parks it there. From there, the rails carry it through a series of machines. First, the car receives a high- pressure washing on both sides. Then soap falls onto the car, like a snowfall. Then three rotating brushes come down, one to each side of the car, and the other on its horizontal surface. Another higher-pressure washing

155

follows, and about a meter further down on the tracks, a drying under the force of pressurized air. Some wets are waiting outside, with spray bottles in one hand, rags in the other. One gets on each side of the car, washing its windshield and wipers, and drying it immediately. Two others get inside, one in the front seat, the other in the back, washing and wiping. Another driver waits to take the car to a spot where a half-dozen more wets are waiting, to finish washing and drying any spots the machine and the other wets missed. In the space of fifteen minutes, the client again sits behind the wheel of a completely clean vehicle.

LEARNING ENGLISH

My morning work schedule is from eight in the morning until one o'clock in the afternoon. During our half hour lunch I always go home, a walk of about five minutes. Afterwards, I work until five in the afternoon. I enroll in a school to learn English and my work schedule allows time for a shower and supper before night classes begin.

The enrollment costs only a quarter; classes are from seven to nine o'clock every week night. Men and women from fifteen to forty are in the classes, but most of them are Orientals. The teachers, all Anglos, don't speak a word of Spanish during the lessons, even though I hear some of them speak it after classes have adjourned. At first, my studies aren't hard. It's easy to learn things like the names of vegetables, kitchen utensils and traffic signs. But after learning a few phrases, the going gets tough. Conjugating verbs is a headache.

On top of the desk in my uncle's apartment, I've piled a mountain of the papers that they give us as homework after each class, but I never really have the opportunity to practice what I've learned in English. Nobody in the apartment speaks English except my uncle, who speaks it only at work. Everybody where I work speaks Spanish. A few times I go downtown and find, along Broadway Avenue, for example, that all the sales clerks are Latins, and they wait on me in Spanish. The street reminds of the Merced market in Mexico City, because outside each shop, somebody waits on the sidewalk to hawk the virtues of the merchandise and to drag customers in by the arm.

In spite of the time that I spend in class, and in spite of the completed papers that I put on my uncle's desk, it's not long before, on two occasions, I realize that I haven't learned anything about English. The first occasion comes when I go into a bar in which the majority of customers are Orientals or whites. Benjamín and I are the only wets. We are sitting at a table drinking our beers when we see a young Oriental girl come in, carrying school books in her arms. She puts them down somewhere behind the bar and then comes to mix with the customers. After a while, she passes next to us and says something to me in English. I don't understand a syllable of it. Benjamín, who more or less understands the language, says that she is asking me if I like to dance. The young girl is short and thin, with wide, dark eyes and short black hair. "I'm not a dancer, but I can move my feet," I say in Spanish. She looks at Benji, thinking that he will translate what I've said, but he says nothing. I stand up and lead her onto the dance floor. Disco music is playing. The dance floor is small and crowded, and the others decide to form a line, women on one side, men on the other. The Oriental girl, on getting in line, is a good distance from me, and all of us men, on my side, are tightly squeezed together. I feel as if there is more danger of falling than opportunity to dance, and I signal to her that I'm going to leave the dance floor. She doesn't follow. A half hour later, as Benjamín and I are leaving the bar, we encounter her in the doorway. She says something to us in English. I have to ask Benjamín what she is saying. He says that she's asking if we're leaving, already.

"Tell her we'll be back in a little while," I say to Benjamín.

He tries, but can't make himself understood. The whole outing becomes a failure when we can't find Benjamín's car. We deduce that the police must have towed it away, because we'd parked in a prohibited zone.

The second time my English studies fail me is in class when the teacher asks me about my job.

"I'm worker," I tell her, thinking that the response is appropriate.

She shakes her head from side to side, negatively, and starts saying some words to make me understand what she is asking, until one of the guys seated beside me in a low voice tells me in Spanish that she wants to know what kind of work I do.

"I'm car washer," I finally say.

THE DOG

One day, I almost get fired from the car wash on account of a dog as big as a bear. At lunchtime, as always, I am walking home wearing my white overalls with my spray bottle hanging from one of its pockets. About two blocks from the car wash, a dog comes out from behind a wall and blocks my path. He is so big that his back comes up to my shoulders and, because he is short-haired, I can see that he is all muscles. His head is about a foot wide. If I had seen him from a block away, I'd have returned to the car wash. When I do see him, my hair stands on end and I feel chills down my back. I keep walking, trying not to show my nervousness, but the animal catches up with me, showing its teeth. I think about running, but it would be useless. He'd catch me in one leap. So I try to stay still, and that, it turns out, is exactly what he wants. He sits down on his rear legs, his head level with mine. He has me at his mercy, if that is what he wants.

After a few minutes, I try to take a step. But the dog shows his teeth and lets out a threatening growl, which I take as an order to stay in my place. I am sweating from nervousness, but I don't dare to move even my head, for fear of being devoured by his big jaws, which certainly are capable of tearing me to pieces or breaking my bones. I shoot my eyes from side to side, looking for a way to call for help, but there is no one and nothing in sight, not even a car. How am I going to defend myself, if there isn't a rock or a stick? All I have for defending myself is my spray bottle, which I figure is of no use. While the dog holds me there, I ask myself why people keep such huge animals, which can't be of any practical use to them. The animal that is guarding me, perfectly healthy and fat, certainly must eat as much as a dozen children in the mountain regions of Oaxaca, and I am sure that he is only a decoration in his house, like a vase for plants or a painting on a wall.

In my village we also keep dogs, not just one, but two or three, but that's because they're good for something. They guard the house against strangers and other dogs, and they keep an eye out for coyotes, who are sometimes bold enough to come right into the chicken houses. They accompany us when we go into the fields, they keep watch on the cattle, and some of them, who have good noses, can follow tracks. They'll put their noses to the ground, then take off running, and bark for us when they've located a deer or an armadillo or a badger.

Twenty minutes pass before an old woman, bent and slow-moving, comes out of the house beyond the wall. In a weak voice that sounds like someone scratching on paper, I hear her say, "Come on, boy!" I do not know if she sees me.

On hearing the call, the dog shoot off towards his mistress, and I breathe a sigh of relief. I go on to the apartment, make a couple of sandwiches, and eat them on my way back to work. But I arrive late, and they've already put another wet in my place. Fortunately, he is a guy who already works at the car wash.

"A few minutes more and I would have hired somebody to take your job," the manager tells me.

I tell him about the dog.

"You should have let him bite you," he says. "Then you could have collected a good bit of insurance from the owner."

ALMOST AMONG THE MISSING

One Saturday afternoon, after we have drunk a few beers with my uncle, Benjamín and I get into his old car in search of adventure. My uncle stays home because he's tired from the work week, and has a job to finish on Sunday. Benjamín goes into a convenience store and comes out with a couple of little vials.

"Let's perfume the heap," he says, opening one of them. The vials are shaped like poppies, and he puts one of them between the headliner and the sun visor.

"The smell will spread, you'll see in just a minute. At least the car will smell good, and who knows, we may seduce a couple of women."

We close the windows so that the fragrance will spread and impregnate rapidly, Benjamín says, sniffing the air every few seconds to test his theory. After a few minutes the fragrance has spread too much, and it smells like caramel mixed with some kind of cheap perfume. It makes me dizzy and there's nothing to do except roll down the windows and let the air carry away the perfume's odor.

"Let's go play billiards," Benjamín says, stopping in front of a little beer joint. It's really only a little hut, barely having space for three tables with four chairs each, and a pool table. In front of the bar are some stools. The place is full of white men, Chicanos, blacks and us wetbacks. We order our beers. I lay a quarter atop our table, betting on a game of pool that's being played, but I lose. A little later, Benjamín bets on his first game and wins. The bartender places in front of us a glass pitcher filled with beer, and Benjamín bets the pitcher on the winner of the last pool game. Benjamín keeps winning and we can barely drink all the pitchers that are brought to our table. The experience that Benjamín has gained over the past year, betting almost every Saturday on the pool games, is giving us free beer, and he keeps winning until about two a.m., when the only people left in the bar are us two wetbacks, one Chicano, one white and one black. We invite the others to sit down and help us drink the pitchers that we haven't been able to finish, until at last, the bartender asks us to leave so that he can close up. But even as we leave, he lets us buy a beer each, to take with us. Benjamín and I stand outside, on one side of the bar, drinking the beers and listening to the others talk in English, but we don't understand anything. After a little while, one of them begins to talk heatedly, and then we see the white man run towards a pickup that is parked on the other side of the street. He opens its door and pulls out a shotgun. We hear the sound of a shell being chambered and, looking around, we see that the Chicano and the black have disappeared in the blinking of an eye.

"Look at the fool!" Benjamín says, as he takes out across an adjacent avenue, where, at this hour, there is almost no traffic.

Holding the shotgun at chest height, the white man heads back to where the group of us had been standing.

"Run! That fool is going to fill you with lead," I hear Benjamín shout to me. By the time I react, the white man is near. All the alcohol I've drunk seems to lose its effect, and in two great leaps I land behind some bushes next to the sidewalk. As I hit ground, I hear the shotgun fire behind me. It hits a tree a few yards away, taking off a spot of bark. I crawl on all fours until I reach the avenue, and run like the devil to cross it. Fortunately, the Anglo has quit following or noticing us. We hadn't offended him, but perhaps on not finding the black and the Chicano, he turned his rage onto us.

"Let's get out of here!" Benjamín says when I reach him.

But the police are on the scene in a minute's time.

We run a couple of blocks down the avenue and go into a restaurant, where we order hamburgers. We hear the siren of another police car and watch as it passes by the restaurant. It stops down the street in front of the beer joint.

With a little bad luck, my name might have been added to the list of my townsmen who have died in California. According to what people in the village say, one of them had been killed by the police. The version generally told is that the deceased was with a group of friends, smoking pot, when they saw the police coming. The deceased villager started running and, although the police shouted for him to stop, he kept running until they shot him. Another was killed supposedly by hoodlums during a party held by some of the townsmen who live in Los Angeles. There's a third guy who is regarded as dead, but whose destiny is actually unknown. He was last seen about four years ago, working as a dishwasher in a restaurant, but since that time, nobody has been able to give account of him. For several months townsmen asked for him in jails, hospitals and even at morgues, but they didn't turn up any trace of Gregorio, who at the time of his disappearance was about twenty-five.

Among our townsmen different stories are told about him. "They've killed him," most people argue, pointing out that he liked to go to bars, and he never left until they closed. Others say that he's in New York, and that they wouldn't be surprised if he returned to California any day. "He'll appear in a while," some of them say, and in the village, they say that he'll show up in a flashy car, with a pretty woman by his side, and, as is almost the custom, he will go into a store and order beer for everybody who comes by. The most worrisome sign is that he has not communicated with his mother, who is still in the village. For about six months, she sent letters to different townsmen in Los Angeles, asking for information, but nobody was able to tell her anything. Even now, whenever anybody comes home from Los Angeles, she goes running to ask about her son. She is still waiting for his return, candle lighted in the village church, praying for his return. In her house she has set aside an altar dedicated to Gregorio, with a big picture of him surrounded by those of her saints of devotion. Almost every day she puts cups of coffee or *atole* on the altar, for his consumption, and on the Day of the Dead, the altar is loaded with foods that he liked. Whenever Gregorio's name is mentioned in townsmens' conversations, everyone recalls that he was a man who was self-confident, that he had played the trumpet in the village band, and that he had won first place in a speed-reading and recitation contest that the director of the primary school organized.

THE INTERNATIONAL GRAPEVINE

In Los Angeles, it's not hard to stay in touch with other townsmen, since almost everybody knows where everybody else lives
and works. I calculate that there are about four hundred of us in
different locales in California: Los Angeles, Santa Monica, Santa
Barbara, El Monte, San Fernando, San Gabriel, Glendale, Rose-
mead, Hollywood, North Hollywood and Encino. Everything that
happens in the village is immediately known, since all of us have
telephones in our apartments or at work. On top of that, almost
every Sunday afternoon groups of us get together at city parks to
compete in improvised basketball games, even though the trophy
for winning teams is often a case of beer, and the whole affair ends
in a binge, especially since there's beer in the refrigerators of all
our homes, and it's usual to invite visitors to drink beers while
they chat. On weekends and on other days off from work, home
visits often end in drunken scenes, too.

Thanks to the free communication between townsmen, we always know who has recently come to California from home and
where the newcomers are staying. When a man arrives, for a few
weeks he greets with beer and food a steady stream of visitors,
who ask about affairs at home. We also know who is planning to
leave soon, and I, for example, take the chance to send a small
electric saw for my family's woodshop, and also some clothing for
my younger brothers.

Among the village youth, those who aren't studying in Mexico
City or Oaxaca City are in the United States as wets. Nor do the
women stay behind. Of the first two young women who came, one
has made her home in Los Angeles and now has children who are
grown and married. The second, by twists of fate, has wound up
living in Tijuana; it is she upon whom the duty falls of helping
townsmen who arrive at the border to find *coyotes* who will take
them north to Los Angeles. A lot of the village women, who used
to earn miserable salaries as maids in Mexico City, are also now
in Los Angeles, doing the same work, but for much better pay.

Though there are a lot of men who are working in the United States and, like my uncle, keeping their families in the village, periodically sending them money orders and visiting them from time to time, there are also a lot who over the course of years have established themselves permanently in the U.S. They came when green cards were easy to get, or they married citizens or green-carders in the States. The majority of these immigrants own their houses, and one of them is now the owner of a house with rooms to rent. They also all have dependable jobs. Some are gardeners with established routes in residential areas, usually in the houses of Anglos whose families own two and even three cars. Some have also become trusted restaurant employees, having worked at the same restaurant for years and having learned a little English, though not enough to speak it completely. These townsmen no longer plan to return to Mexico. Their families have grown and their children are attending American public schools. Aside from the family of the first woman who came, the first American citizen to be the child of wetbacks is a young man who is now twenty years old.

Given the great number of townsmen who are in the United States, it has been possible to help the village economically when it has been in difficult straits, as when recently a short circuit in electric cables caused a fire in the Juárez mountains of Oaxaca, burning away a good bit of the communal forest lands of our village and others. When that happened, all it took was one telephone call from the village, and a day later everyone in California knew about the blazes. One of the California townsmen immediately went to everybody's home or job to collect money which was sent to the village authorities. The authorities used it to buy shovels and picks, hatchets and other tools, and food for those who were fighting the fire day and night. Day after day telephone calls brought news about the fire, although in process of being passed from mouth to mouth the news was exaggerated a bit. It was said, for example, that the fire had grown so big that its ferocious tongues reached the village and burned a few houses, and that the chief of communal properties and two others had been trapped in the middle of the blaze. For a day, all of us in the California community believed that they had died, but then we learned that they had reappeared so caked with carbon that no one recognized them. During their odyssey, it was said that the three had taken refuge in a little creek that runs at the foot of the mountains and that several times they'd had to lower themselves into its waters when the tongues of fire had come too close. The truth, it turned out, was that they had been cut off from others who were fighting the fire, and that they were

disoriented and had run in the wrong direction. It took them a day
to get their bearings, and they had nothing to eat, but otherwise,
they were not subject to any harm.

Little by little, as events like the fire passed, the idea grew
among us townsmen of forming an organization whose job would
be to stay in constant contact with the village authorities. We
formed a committee with elective officers which called itself OPAM,
or "*Organización Pro Ayuda a Macuiltianguis,*" the Organization
for Aid to Macuiltianguis. To raise funds, the organization spon-
sors monthly dances, raffles and collections. It wasn't long before
the organization was able to help. After general discussion and
agreement, it sent a movie projector to the village with a townsman, who didn't have to pay taxes to import it to Mexico, because
as soon as it was formed, the leaders of OPAM had gone to the
Mexican consulate to get the consul's help with the customs service. Following a long and less serene discussion, Macuil's diasporans also sent a quantity of dollars for distribution among village
oldsters and widows. The group also sends money to finance village celebrations, such as the day of St. Paul every December 25;
the celebration is essentially a two-day basketball tournament to
which every town in the region sends its best team.

CARNIVAL REMEMBERED

The California organization also contributes to Mardi Gras or Carnival, celebrated on the four days preceding Ash Wednesday. Carnival, as the celebration is called, is a festival that used to be the responsibility of the village's Society of the Young, but now, everybody takes a responsibility, because so few young people remain in the village. During the four festival days, nobody works and the schools close. Four bulls are made for the festival, three of them life-size, and a smaller one, for the children. All four are made of the branches of the bush we call "Galinda Paz" that grows in the hills outside of town. The bush grows tall, straight and without many branches. When heated, the branches can be doubled without breaking. The limbs and ribs of the bulls are formed with these branches, along a backbone made of a thick plank of pine. The skeletons are then covered with straw mats; then eyes, ears and a long tongue are added with red paint. On one side of each bull, the letters MC are painted, imitating the brand used on all townsmen's cattle to prevent confusion with animals belonging to other villages. The bulls are also painted with the names each is given for the festival. Among the names I recall is "Lucio Cabañas," the real name of a guerrilla who was operating in the state of Guerrero at the time. Another time, a bull was named "The Foreign Debt." By Saturday, when festivities start, the bulls should be ready, and the town authorities are expected to have on hand enough *tepache*, a beverage made from fermented maguey or sugar cane. The authorities, each in his turn, are expected to toast the villagers and be toasted with glasses or gourds of *tepache*. The musicians must also be ready to play the sounds that we call "Stupidities" in the village.

The young people very early in the day prepare to go out of their homes disguised in masks as old people. Many of the young men dress as women, using clothing lent to them by their girlfriends, or anybody willing to make the sacrifice, because it's certain that their costumes will be in tatters by the time the celebrations are done. The women and children dress in new clothing for dances, and children are usually given a few pesos in case they want to buy candies. Adults and young people dance to the "Stupidities" the musicians play, and a few agile people carry the bulls on their shoulders, trying to knock the dancers off their feet. Their usual victims are those who've had too much *tepache*, and among them, not a few are left with bruised faces, sprained ankles or broken collarbones. Disguised people change their voices while they're in public view; those dressed as women speaking in falsetto, and those dressed as old people talk in guttural voices.

Everyone bullfights, trying to hit the bulls as they pass. "Over here are the springy people," or "We don't bend or break," people shout at the bulls, taunting them to charge. At the end of each day, those dressed as old folks have to compose verses. They are permitted to talk about other people, about the authorities, about girlfriends and boyfriends and rumors they've heard since the last carnival. From time to time, some people among the spectators are offended, and they come out onto the "battlefield," as the dance floor is called, to trade blows with those in disguise; and sometimes all the parties to such scuffles wind up spending the night in jail for having disturbed the public order. The bulls frequently have to be recovered with straw mats, because the mats they wear get torn off by spectators. This goes on for four days, until on the final night of the festival, the bulls are burned, and everyone comes onto the dance floor.

Serious accidents aren't common at carnival time, although a few have been known. One of the best remembered came about when a villager wanted to make a great show. On one of his trips to the villages in the interior of the mountain range, he'd bought a type of cape made of palm leaves that is used as a raincoat. The man's idea was that at the end of Carnival, he'd set the cape on fire and run onto the dance floor. The cape he wore is called "a chicken cape" because of the way in which the palm leaves are sewn, and the man had called the act he planned to stage "*verah llih*," or the flaming chicken. He set the cape on fire and began running around, but when he wanted to remove it, in his panic he couldn't undo the knot that held it around his neck. The spectators weren't alarmed until the cape set his clothing on fire and he began yelling. Someone threw a pitcher of *tepache* onto the man, in an effort to put out the fire; but it only made it burn faster. The villager was badly blistered and burned, and the following day, he died.

A PROMOTION

At the car wash, when the supervisors learn that I am taking English, they give me a promotion, even though it comes without an increase in pay. They move me to the gasoline station that is located on the same property. It's an easier job because all I have to do is pump gasoline and make out the ticket for payment at the cash register, and even that's easy, since almost all our business is done on the basis of credit cards. After that, they transfer me to a job as a cleaning man on the part of the lot where we return the cars to their owners. I have to look for places the machines or windshield-washing men have missed, brush the tires and polish the rims. It's a hot job, drying and cleaning, but the sweating gives me pleasure, because there's not a single owner who doesn't tip at least a quarter when his car is returned. On sunny Sundays, as many as a thousand cars may pass through, and on days like that, I go home with the pockets of my overalls bulging with change, sometimes amounting to more than my daily wages.

From time to time, cars filled with teenage Chicanos pass by on the street that runs by the car wash, and as if it were a joke, their occupants shout to us, "Lookout! Here comes *La Migra!*" always in false alarm. It's as if they want to see us go running around, looking for holes in which to hide, like rabbits. Those who have worked here for some time tell us that it's just a local joke, although once, years ago, the *Migra* did come. Its men blocked off all the exits from the car wash, and several guys were taken all the way to Tijuana wearing their overalls.

LIFE AT THE APARTMENT

My fortyish roommate, Antonio, says that he has backaches from having harvested wood with his chain saw in the communal forest at home. Whenever he has a busy day at the restaurant where he works, he comes home complaining of back pains.

"Just look at the way things are, boys," he says one night as we're all watching television just before going to bed. "Back in the village, I won't wash even a dish, but here I live by wrestling with glasses, pots, casserole dishes and frying pans that are loaded with grease."

"You wanted dollars, didn't you?" Benjamín responds.

"Well, yeah, to make dollars."

"Who decided that you had to be poor?" Rubén asks, making fun of Antonio's complaint.

"Well, somebody did, only God knows who," Antonio says, squeezing his waist with both hands and turning around.

"You still haven't gotten well?" my uncle asks.

"I think that I'm going to hurt this way for the rest of my life," Antonio says, in pain.

"It's age, you're an old man, brother," Benjamín tells him laughingly. "The only trouble is, nobody is going to retire you."

"Retire? I hadn't even thought of it. All I'm going to get is a kick in the ass, and somebody saying, 'Goodbye, Tony.' My sons are the only ones who will take care of me."

"Sons?" Rubén asks. "What sons? You've only got one boy, the rest are girls, and as soon as the rooster crows, they'll be married. Then it will be, 'Goodbye, daddy, one of these days we'll bring your grandchildren to visit you.'"

Antonio announces that he's going into the bathroom, and as is his custom every time he comes home tried from work, he takes out a jar that he keeps under his bed, filled with medicinal herbs that are soaked in alcohol. After spending about an hour in a hot bath, he rubs the home remedy over his whole body, and according to what he says, it helps relieve his pain. The smell of the herbs is strong, and it impregnates the whole apartment. It isn't a bad smell, but it gives Rubén a pretext to keep heckling Antonio.

"So there you go with your witches herbs, eh? That won't do you any good. If you'd smoke a joint of marijuana, you'd be better off because you'd forget the pain, and even your name."

"No, I won't do it, none of that," Antonio tells him. "I won't do it. For me, a little *mescal*, nothing more. I don't want any pot."

"That's fine with me," Rubén says, "but when you've finished perfuming yourself with that stuff, open the windows, will you?"

The television set we are watching is a new one my uncle has just bought. It's a color TV, with remote control.

"Look at this," my uncle says, pressing buttons on a machine in his hand. The screen changes channels. "What novelties the darned *gringos* offer us! I'm going to take this tv back to the village."

"That's a good idea," Rubén comments. "We can amaze everybody."

After pushing a few more buttons, my uncle returns the screen to the program we were watching. It is a cowboy movie starring Pedro Infante.

"Yesterday I went to the movies," Benjamín comments. "I went to see a movie about wetbacks. But I got so mad, I left."

"Just what did you see?" my uncle asks.

"Well, a wetback, or really, a handsome Mexican actor playing the part. The movie was about how this wetback goes to a ranch and they give him work and he seduces the owner's daughter and they get married. You know, it had a happy ending. Just imagine me seducing the restaurant owner's daughter and ending up marrying her. Hah! She's good-looking and white! But where do such things happen? Where in the devil do they get ideas for movies like that?"

"It's all a joke," my uncle says.

"Well, let them have their jokes, but I'm not paying four dollars just to get mad again."

One evening, about seven o'clock there's a kettle cooking over the flames of the stove. It's filled with the makings of our supper for the night, a beef stew with canned green chile sauce, pieces of celery, chopped onion, garlic and carrots. My uncle, whose turn it is to do the cooking, has also added powdered oregano and black pepper, a mix of all kinds of things that gives off a pleasant aroma.

"It's okay to put anything in a stew," my uncle says, jokingly. "Who is to say that we won't discover a new Mexican dish? We can give the recipe to Rubén and he can sell it to the restaurant owner, how about that?"

As he's talking the telephone rings. He runs to answer it. I hear him excitedly asking questions: "Where?" "When?" "With who?" "What a mess, man!" "Well, it doesn't matter now. Look, go immediately to Doña Chela's house and don't worry, we'll wait for you here."

Then my uncle gives us the news.

It was Rubén and Benjamín. Earlier in the day they had gone downtown to look around. While they were at a bus stop, on their way home, a couple of *Migra* agents picked them up. They were calling from Tijuana. My uncle tells us not to worry much because, he says, within three days, at the latest, the two will be back in the apartment again.

"How much do you have saved?" my uncle asks Antonio, who is sitting in the bedroom watching television.

"About two hundred dollars," Antonio says.

I've got some money saved, and my uncle, too. We have enough to hire a *coyote* to bring them back. Nothing more is said about the affair.

JAYWALKING

Almost nobody brings his car to be washed when weather fore-
casts call for rain, and nobody comes when it's raining. During the
rainy season there is very little work, so little that the supervisor
has to divide the hours among the workers, reducing the person-
nel to a quarter of those employed on sunny days. There is even
one period of about ten days in which almost nobody is hired because of rains, and the owner, an Anglo, orders the manager to
give us each a check for twenty dollars, "So that they can at least
buy the week's groceries," the manager says. On several days, they
give us a few hours of work just so that we won't be completely
unemployed, and on those days we spend our time cleaning the
brick walls and the windows, time and again, just so that when the
manager looks, he sees us working.

I spend my idle time just walking around town, feeling as miserable as the weather. The city is a boring place to walk when
you're out of work, and it almost costs me fourteen dollars in a
fine for violating the laws about walking. It's not that I don't understand the electric sign that says "Walk" on green or "Wait" on
red, and it isn't the first time that I ignore those signs, because I
prefer to watch for traffic. I've always done this, in Houston, San
Antonio and in Los Angeles, until I walk across the street in view
of a patrolman. At least, I tell myself, in the United States the laws
are respected, unlike in Mexico City, in which you've got to cross
the street dodging between cars in the hopes that, violating a law
himself, some driver doesn't turn you into a billiard ball and sink
you.

I was walking about Los Angeles confidently when, despite the
sign saying to wait, I started across a street. I hadn't reached the
other side when I heard the sound of a siren behind me. But I
didn't think that it could be for me, so I kept walking. A few steps
later, a big, fat cop in a blue uniform, wearing dark glasses and a
helmet, blocked my path on his motorcycle.

"Stop there!" he said. I more or less understood the order.

"Do you speak English?" he asked me right away.

"Some," I told him, lying.

He then recited for me a series of phrases that I didn't understand, but it didn't take much English to realize that what I'd done was kept walking, when the sign said "Wait."

"Where are you from?" he said.

I understood that question, because it had been the first phrase I'd learned on arriving here, and recently, I'd even learned to write it. I didn't know what to answer, and for a minute, I felt sure that he'd take me to *La Migra*. But then I remembered what one of my townsmen had told me. He'd been driving, and maybe because he looked suspicious, or like a wetback, a patrolman had followed him all the way to the restaurant where the townsman worked. In the parking lot the cop had asked to see my townsman's green card and my townsman had told him that, "It's none of your business," although he did show his driver's license. The cop hadn't taken him to *La Migra*, after all.

The agent, noticing that I wasn't saying anything, asked me for identification. I took out my billfold and gave him a false identification card that I'd bought in San Antonio.

To my surprise, it worked.

"From Texas, eh?" he said to himself.

"Yeah," I told him.

Then he took out a notebook that he carried in one of his big pants pockets and began to write, copying my false name onto it.

"Where are you living?" he asked.

When he saw me hesitating, he said, "Hotel?"

"Yes," I told him.

He said something else which I more or less understood that he was asking for the address of the hotel. Maybe I was lucky that I was wearing a backpack in which I had a pair of shoes that I'd bought a half-hour before; I must have looked like a traveler. But I didn't know the name of any hotel. I looked from one side of the street to another.

"There?" he said, pointing towards an old sign that said "Hotel."

"Yes," I told him, and he seemed satisfied.

Then he handed me a sheet of paper with writing in carbon. He went away and I kept walking in peace.

Maybe the police in Los Angeles are used to seeing people come in from Texas, just the way cops in Mexico City are used to seeing people come in from Oaxaca. But the difference is that in Mexico

City when they stop you, they always go through your pockets, searching for something to appropriate.

IDLE HOURS

When you're walking down the streets of downtown Los Angeles, you've got to evade all the touts with their, "Come on in, countrymen, we have this and that, very high quality and very low prices." The truth is, they do have a lot of merchandise, but its quality is doubtful. I know because a co-worker told me that he'd bought a radio/cassette player downtown that with a week's use began to rise and fall in volume by itself, and when he tried to return it, he learned that it had no warranty. Sometimes when I'm downtown I run into unfortunate wetbacks who look tired, with their eyes down, dirty, saying that they've slept in the bus station, or sometimes, in the streets, without work, without money and probably without having eaten in a good while. They ask passersby to help them saying "with whatever you can give me, comrade." When I see them I remember being in almost the same situation in Houston, I give them a dollar, and they seem to appreciate it.

On afternoons when I have absolutely nothing to do, sometimes I go to the ninety-nine cent movies on Broadway street, in old, smelly movie houses whose seats are deteriorated, and where, at times, one can see roaches and even rats scurrying in the shadows. At other times I lose myself in the never-ending world of commerce, looking at a million kinds of merchandise, but I'm only able to buy a shirt or t-shirt. I spend hours looking in hardware stores, staring at ever-more sophisticated machines made to save human labor, and I imagine what wonders we could work if we had such machinery in our wood shop. Though the merchandise is close to my hands, it's far from my purchasing power, and most of the time, I wind up buying only a simple hand tool, to add to the lot that I plan to take home when I go.

At other times, I walk among the skyscrapers, many of which have glass walls through which the sun is reflected by day, and the lights of the city by night, when they appear to be grand guardians, watching over the city's sleep. Sometimes, when leaving the deserted downtown area late at night, I feel as if I'm the last human

176

being left in a world of buildings and machines. As I walk the long blocks between buildings, I also feel smaller. On one of side of me I see buildings, buildings and more buildings, and on the other, nothing but cars; no one walks in the city at late hours. Once or twice cars pass me and from inside them, someone yells out something like, "*Adiós Mojado*," or "Goodbye Wetback," but since the voice disappears immediately as the cars pass by at great speed, I am left with the impression that the cars themselves shouted at me.

HARVEST BOUND

On days when there is work, I talk to the other guys. Some of them tell me that the harvest season is coming in northern California, and they say that one can earn good money there. Things haven't gone so badly in the car wash, but one afternoon I give the manager my thanks for having hired and promoted me, and with a little suitcase that night I board a Greyhound headed north. My ticket is made out for San Francisco, but I don't plan to go that far. I plan to ride until I find a place where people are harvesting, and to get off the bus there.

I sleep on the bus for a few hours that night, and in the morning, when I awake, I don't know where we are. I get up from my seat and walk down the bus aisle, looking for a Mexican or Chicano to tell me our location, but oddly enough, I don't see any among the passengers, who are all white-skinned. I pay attention to the road signs we pass, but they are not of much help. I can read the town names, but I don't know where the towns lie. A map would help me, and I decide to buy one at our next stop. Lots of things are for sale at the bus stop's gift shop, but there are no maps. I direct myself towards the shop's operator, but I run into the language barrier. The operator is an Anglo, and when I speak to him in Spanish, he says that he doesn't understand. I try to practice my very precarious English with him, but it's of no use. I have a rough idea of the sound of the words that I want to say, but I can't pronounce them right. I make signs, signaling a big piece of paper and say "from California," but he turns into a question mark, with eyes wide open, arms raised and hands extended. "Map," I say, but I don't pronounce the word very well. "Freeways, streets," I add, but he still doesn't understand. He points out chewing gum, candies, pieces of cake, sandwiches, soft drinks, and cigarettes, trying to guess what I'm asking for. But he doesn't show me any maps. Finally, I back out of the store, and as I leave I hear him say, "I'm sorry."

A little before the bus leaves, I run into a Mexican- American in a hallway and I immediately ask him to help me find a map of California. We go back to the store. The Chicano asks for a map. "Ahh! Ahaaa!" the operator exclaims. Then he goes to a corner of his shelves and takes out what I'd been asking for. While I am paying him, he talks to the Chicano in a joyful tone. With the map in my hands, I give the Chicano my thanks, and he explains that the storekeeper thought that I was asking if he needed anybody to clean the floor or "mop."

IN MY FATHER'S FOOTSTEPS

The bus advances into extensive plains, so extensive that you can't see where they end. All of the land is cultivated, perfectly clean of plants and perfectly plowed in straight lines that seem to open out before the bus, like a fan extending itself. Soon, we are passing by big vineyards and fields of onion, beets, avocado, tomatoes and other types of fruits and vegetables, so many that I assume that the harvests will be in tons.

Back at home, villagers also plant these types of crops, but only for family consumption, and from time to time, to sell to neighbors. My mother has for years kept and supervised such a garden on a plot by our house. She knows what to plant, depending upon the climate, whether in times of hot or cold, rain or snowfall. My brothers and I prepare the seed beds in our off- hours after school. In addition to vegetables, our garden has apple, plum, peach, cherry, avocado and pecan trees.

My father also traveled the immense plains of California, "bending his back," as he put it, during his time as a *bracero*. Once when we were weeding our cornfield, he told my younger brother and I the story of a tomato harvest here. At the time that dad told the story, my younger brother wasn't big enough to use the *coa* to weed. Instead, he pulled weeds with his hands, and, as I recall, spent most of his effort chasing after the crickets he found in his path.

My father said that in California, the rows of fields were long and perfectly flat, like those I see through the window of the bus. But when he described the plains for us, because there are no such lands near our village, we weren't sure we believed him. I remember looking on a map, to see if his description could be true, but all I could tell from looking at it was that California was a long way from home.

My father said that among the foremen who were hired by the contractor was a type of trainer. His job was teaching the newly arrived *braceros* how to work at the speed the company wanted.

All the *braceros* feared him. He was a tall man, as thin as a rail. He wore cowboy boots, had a big moustache, wore a wide-brimmed hat and had a stare of steel. His name was Pierre, but the *braceros* nicknamed him "*El Perro*," "The Dog." He was so demanding that nobody could for long keep the pace he wanted. Whenever he came near, somebody would say, "Here comes the Dog," and as word passed, everybody would start working at full speed. But there was no way to satisfy him. At first, he only insulted them: "Bend over, lazy, you've come here to work, so get to work!" When he was watching, nothing distracted him. If a *bracero* stood up to stretch and rub his back, The Dog immediately blew a whistle, and made a signal— by raising his hand and doubling his index finger—to show the bracero that he should bend back to his work. Of course there were a few rebels who refused to obey, but they ran the risk of being laid off for a couple of days while they "recuperated"— the company said—from their strains, or worse, of having their contracts cancelled and being returned to Mexico, as a few men were.

Only the contractor admired the foreman, since the foreman squeezed maximum productivity out of his *braceros*. Among the *braceros*, no one liked the foreman, though they obeyed him. One day a man from Querétaro, whom the others called the Queretano, a short, thin and quick-witted fellow, stopped in the middle of a row to rub his back. Then he and another *bracero* started pushing against one another, each one trying to topple the other, all in an effort to rest and distract themselves a minute. The Dog blew his whistle immediately, but only one of the men bent over the row again. The Queretano stayed on his feet, stretching. The Dog whistled a second time; a second whistle, he had taught the men, meant that the offending worker had to take off the rest of the day. The Queretano, without showing any fear, but also without trying to be offensive, shouted, "Why do you dog us so much? We're not machines. You should come out here with us, for just one row, so that you can feel like we do."

The Dog ordered him to take the day off, and that meant, without pay. The Queretano had to obey, but everybody admired him for having spoken up in the way he did. Everyone warned him to be on guard, because the next time the Queretano said anything to the Dog, he risked being sent back to Mexico.

Instead of being frightened, the Queretano proposed to his friends an idea for getting even with the Dog. Several days passed before his friends agreed, because even the closest of them warned against any action that might get them returned, since getting the contracts had not been easy, in the first place. But finally, they all consented. One day at lunch, to the surprise of the field crew, they heard the Dog yelling curses inside his pickup, where he was accustomed to eat at a distance from the *braceros.* "Those sons of whores!" they heard him exclaim. Then they saw him walking towards them, still cursing and, my father said, with saliva dripping from his mouth. His fists were doubled and his eyes shot sparks. He went group-to-group among the *braceros,* asking who had played the trick on him, but no one said anything.

The Queretano's idea had been to simply go to the foreman's pickup, throw out his lunch, and put in its place in his lunch pail a note saying, "Dog, go fuck your mother."

"All of us were glad to see that the trick had infuriated the Dog, but we were also afraid he'd discover its origins," Dad had told us. "But thanks be to God," he added, "nobody said anything." The Queretano had broken the immaculate authority of the Dog. The trick had gained the respect of all the *braceros,* even though most of them weren't sure whether the Queretano or one of his friends had played it.

But, to take his own vengeance, the Dog became even more demanding and punitive. His ferocity grew bolder by the day. After a week or two of this harsher treatment, the Queretano proposed that everybody throw tomatoes at the Dog. "And after that, we'll have to pack our bags," one of the *braceros* told him. "The contractor won't forgive us if we treat his best foreman like that," another one said. But little by little, the idea grew popular.

The plan was for the Queretano to stand in the middle of the field, scratching himself, to attract the foreman's attention, while everyone else continued working at a fast pace. When the foreman saw the Queretano standing, he shouted, "What has happened to you today, you son of a whore? Are you sick? Or do you want at least a week of layoff? Doesn't it make you ashamed to see everybody else working?" The Queretano withstood several insults, until the appropriate moment, when the Dog came out into the middle of the field, where the Queretano was standing. Then one of the workers behind the Dog rose up and threw an overripe tomato, hitting the Dog in the back. The Dog turned and looked and, seeing no one, fell upon the Queretano. But when he did, he was hit again, and again from the backside. Before long, tomatoes were raining upon the Dog, who could do nothing but run. As he ran back towards the edge of the field, several times he tripped and fell on tomato plants. Everything had gone according to plan.

By the time he reached his pickup, his clothing was badly spotted from the tomato attack. He got in his pickup and went roaring off. The *braceros* lost sight of him in the dust he left behind. Then, rapidly, the others helped the Queretano catch-up on the row he'd been working when he had stopped. They did that in order to show the contractor that they knew how to work, without the foreman's insults. When the contractor came a little later in the afternoon, he saw that the work had advanced at a normal rate, and when he couldn't find the Dog, he asked a *bracero* what had become of the foreman. The *bracero* pointed in the direction in which the foreman had gone. The contractor drove off to find him. He came back about an hour later. Everybody expected an exemplary punishment and some were sure that they'd all be sent home. But the contractor merely watched, until quitting time came. Then he spoke to the crowd of them. "So that's what you did to Pierre, eh? Nobody liked him, I already knew that. You guys were within your rights." Then he told them that he had found the Dog down the road a mile or two, bent over the steering wheel of his pickup, crying with rage. The contractor said that he'd told the foreman not to come back to work.

RIPON

As the bus comes into a town called Ripon, I see five men walking on the sidewalk, men who, by their style of dress, I take to be wetbacks on their way to work. Their clothes are stained with dirt, just like their caps and tennis shoes. The bus goes into the little town's business district and stops at a little wooden building bearing the name of the bus line. Without thinking much, I grab my suitcase and get off. Estimating my route, I walk back towards the place where I'd seen the wets, but am unable to find them. On one side of the road where I'm standing, I see ahead of me houses that look like those in Hispanic neighborhoods, and on the other side of the road, nicer, walled-in houses of brick, which I take to be houses where Anglos live. I walk towards the Latin settlement. It's a small place, with only one store. I run into a wetback who is leaving the store, carrying a bag of groceries, and I ask him where I can find work.

"The truth, friend, is that I don't know where," he answers me. "I'm trimming the vineyards, but we've only got work until tomorrow. The work we're doing is about to be finished."

"And you don't know where else I can ask?"

"I don't know that, either. A lot of people have come to the contractor I'm working for, and he's sent them away."

I am not worried, even though the news is not encouraging, because if worst comes to worst, I can buy a ticket and go back to Los Angeles.

But I can't understand why I had stopped in such a small town, and not in a city. Maybe it was because I'm from a small town and hang onto the idea that small town people are friendly. At least that's the way my village treats outsiders, when they don't offend us. In my village, nobody refuses an outsider a bowl of beans, or at least a snack. There's even a saying, "Food is sacred and you should not refuse it to anyone." On the other hand, in a city, everyone is indifferent to everyone else. I walk up and down the neighborhood and run into other Mexicans, but they all give

184

similar reports; work is not to be had. After a while I realize that the sun is going down, and that I've got nowhere to stay for the night.

As darkness comes, the streets clear and I no longer find people to ask about work. I go into the store and buy a packaged hamburger. The storekeeper heats it in his microwave oven, and I go outside to eat it while walking. Now and then a car passes by. I walk back down to the bus station, but after about an hour, its caretaker locks the place to go home, and once again I'm without anywhere to stay. In the distance, I see the yellow sign of a gasoline station. I go towards it. Luckily, it's warm and I figure that I won't have to suffer from a cold night. I can lay down on a corner of the station's driveway, and the heat that the concrete has stored by day will warm me. About ten o'clock at night a station wagon pulls in to get gasoline. A short man of about twenty-five gets out. He goes into the office, comes back onto the driveway and unhooks the hose from the gas pump. Somebody inside the car hands him a key with which he opens the gas cap. Then he puts the hose in and begins pumping.

I get up from my improvised sleeping place, planning to ask the man where I might find work. I realize that asking that question at such a late hour may cause him to laugh at me, but I've got nothing to lose, after all.

On seeing me approach, the man at the pump changes his aspect from that of a self-confident man to one who is standing guard. He stares at me for a minute and then pretends not to pay any attention. When I ask him, he only shakes his head negatively. I decide not to ask any more questions, because at this hour, anything one might ask gives rise to suspicions.

As I am walking away, I hear women talking and giggling inside the car. They are talking in Spanish, but from my distance, I cannot understand them.

Very early the next day, I start my search again and after a few hours, I encounter a wetback from the state of Puebla. He tells me that there is work, but there are too many workers. For the past two months, he says, he's been here, working only two or three days a week, because there's not enough work for everyone. Then he directs me towards a house where a family from Puebla lives. The family has been in the United States for about ten years, he says, and its members know the contractors who take people to work in the countryside.

The house is of wood and without any fence, like all of the houses in the Hispanic neighborhood. Here and there in its yard are decorative plants. A child is riding a rusted tricycle on the lawn, and two others are making mounds of dirt with their hands. They don't pay much attention when they see me, but look at each other, as if each were expecting the others to speak. None of them says anything.

There is no closed door upon which to knock. Instead, there's a rusted and torn screen door, ajar. I say, "*Buenos días*," to attract attention. A woman of about forty, dressed in worn, cheap clothes, comes to the door. Her hair is tied above her head with a faded red bandanna.

"Yes?" she says, leaning out the doorway.

I ask for Señor Pepe Zavala, as the wetback I encountered told me to do.

"Who wants to see him and how do you happen to know him?" she says, suspiciously. "He's not here right now," she adds.

I tell her how I was directed to her house, and that I arrived in town the day before, looking for work.

"Well, *el señor* won't be back until about eight o'clock tonight," she tells me. Just as with others, I ask her to advise me where I might find a job, explaining that I know nobody in town. Once again, I hear the same answers.

Her mistrust eases, and she steps out onto on the porch. I notice that her face is sunburned and her hands are calloused.

"I imagined that it was easier to find work," I tell her, just to have something to say to prolong the conversation.

"Over there in Los Angeles, you hear that in this area harvest time is due, and they say that people make good money."

"Sure, it's true, one can make a good bit when one is lucky enough to work good land," she says. "Where are you from?"

"From Oaxaca."

"And you don't know anybody here?"

"No."

"And you came all the way here, just trusting in God! There are a lot like you, and every year, more of them."

Behind her appears another woman, about twenty, with a rounded face, like hers. The younger woman is a little chubby. On seeing me, she opens her eyes wide.

"Mother!" she says to the older woman. "This is the guy that we ran into at the gas station!"

"Are you sure?"

"Yes! Did you spend the night at the station?" the younger one asks, incredulity in her voice.

"Yes," I tell them. "I spent the night there. The good thing is, the weather isn't cold."

"What a barbarity!" the older woman exclaims. "And I imagine that you haven't eaten."

"Not eating hasn't bothered me. I've just gotten into town, and I came prepared," I say.

"Well, come on in," the mother says. "Last night the girls came in and told me that they had seen a young man sleeping at the gas station. That bothered us, but we have to be careful, because you can't take risks with strangers. My husband is Señor Zavala, and he does know the contractors. Maybe he can take you on," the mother continues. "There's not much work, but at least you can earn enough to stay alive. Come on in, and when night comes, you can go across the street, where we've rented a place in which other people from Puebla are staying. There aren't any beds, but at least you'll have a roof over your head."

I tell the mother and daughter that I appreciate their attention.

Inside the house, beneath the peaked tin roof, are a series of small rooms. On entering, you come into a living room whose wooden walls are unadorned except for a coat of white paint. A couple of old wine-colored sofas stand against a wall, facing a low table on which a color television sits. The cement floor is covered with a dirty rug of the same color as the sofas. The living room opens onto a kitchen with all the appliances, stove, refrigerator, dish washer. On one wall of the kitchen hang several kitchen utensils and platters and some keys. Beyond the kitchen are the bath and three small bedrooms.

The mother and daughter tell me that the work available now is trimming in the vineyards and thinning in the tomato fields. They say that they came to Ripon from Puebla ten years ago as renters, but that they now own the house where they live. Since settling-in, they say they've helped others from Puebla and a few disoriented people like me. Their own house grew too small for those they were aiding, so they've begun renting the house across the street for three hundred dollars a month. They say that from ten to fifteen wets usually stay there, paying two dollars a day.

The house across the street is in about the same condition as their own, except that it doesn't have as many divisions, and it has no furniture, only piles of dirty blankets and a bathroom with a commode and shower. Behind the house the grass has grown tall in the yard.

That afternoon the inhabitants of both houses arrive in two old, but big cars. One of the cars is the one that I'd seen the night before at the gas station. Sixteen people get out of the two cars, among them two middle-aged women. Right away the mother and daughter introduce me to the father, telling him how I've come to the house. He greets me in a friendly way and says that we'll be going into the countryside to work at five in the morning.

Mr. Zavala's older son, about thirty years old, drives one of the station wagons. He lives in Stockton, and he leaves shortly after arriving at the house. Mr. Zavala's daughter, her husband, also about twenty, and their two schoolchildren live in the house with Mr. Zavala and his wife. Thirteen people are living in the workers' house; I am the fourteenth. Mrs. Zavala tells me that if I'd like, she can prepare tacos for me to take to lunch tomorrow. I accept her offer with pleasure.

GRAPES AND TOMATOES

Among the tenants in the workers' house is a twenty- three-year-old from Puebla who says that he has recently graduated from normal college. When I ask him why he's come to the United States, he says that he just wanted to see the world before assuming his profession. He always carries—even at work in the fields—a radio/cassette player, with tapes of *ranchera* music. Another tenant is a young man of fourteen from Mexico City whom the others call "*El Chilango*," a nickname derisive of the capital. The rest of the tenants are middle-aged peasants from Mr. Zavala's hometown.

There are enough blankets for everybody. At five in the morning, after throwing cold water on our faces to break our sleepiness, we run to Mr. Zavala's house and get into the cars, which are already waiting. Mrs. Zavala hands everybody a lunch wrapped in aluminum paper. After driving over dirt roads for about twenty minutes, we come to the vineyards. They give us each a pair of scissors and point out to each of us a row. Mrs. Zavala shows me what I must do. The vines are about five feet tall, planted at prudent distances along a straight row. Their branches grow up and down on a fence of wires. My job is to cut those shoots that have grown low, along the ground, and high, above the fence, and also to remove those branches that have died. The foreman passes by constantly, inspecting the work that we've done. At lunch, people gather in small groups under the shade of the vines. Our tacos are of beans and egg. The eight hour workday passes quickly, and at the end of it, I'm told that the wage scale is three dollars and thirty-five cents an hour.

For a month we work regularly in the vineyards, four days a week. After that, they take us to the tomato fields for thinning. For that job they give us long-handled hoes. The work consists of killing the plants that have grown too much, and thinning out extra plants so that they are spaced about five inches apart.

Every week I pay Mrs. Zavala ten dollars for the lunches she prepares, and for the times that I have breakfast or dinner with her family.

The town doesn't have any entertainment centers, and although
Stockton does have some, none of the tenants has a car. On days
when there's no work, some people play soccer in the front yard
and others drink beer. A couple of times, young women pull up
in cars to offer their services as prostitutes. One of the guys tells
me that about a month ago, a blonde came by and offered to sleep
with all of them, one at a time. They accepted her offer. But the
guy who tells me the story says that he was the last in line, and
that her nipples bled. Nobody knew if it was because she'd taken
on too many men, or because, perhaps, she was ill, and they all
spent several weeks afterwards worrying that they'd contracted a
disease. But fortunately, no one noticed any symptoms.

The Zavala family spends most of its free time watching
Spanish-language television programs. On Sundays, a mini-bus
comes to their house and takes them to the Pentecostal church in
Stockton, which they joined on coming to the United States. Mrs.
Zavala praises the church members for having influenced her hus-
band to give up beer, which he used to drink every weekend.

OREGON

About two weeks after my arrival, the Zavala family begins planning to work further north. They say that for several years they've earned good wages in the cherry harvests in Oregon. The week before leaving, they take their cars to a mechanic for a general review. All of us tenants are invited to go along, and we are offered transportation to Oregon and back. The Zavalas also tell us that we won't have to pay for the ride until we've been paid for our first jobs in Oregon. "The work there is a sure thing," Mr. Zavala's son tells us. "If you want to, and if you know how to work, you can come back driving a car, a used but good one, because up there you can buy them cheaply." There's no limit on the number who can go; all of us volunteer. From the Zavala family, only the daughter stays, to keep watch on the young children.

Altogether, five vehicles make the trip: two from Ripon and three from Stockton. I get into the rear of a white van from which the seats have been removed; six of us sit on top of some blankets and kitchen equipment that belongs to the Zavalas. Two more ride in front, including the driver, whom I've never seen before. He's a long-haired, dark-skinned Hispanic, dressed in denim pants, shirt and jacket, with high-topped, laced boots. "He's going to be one of our foremen," one of the tenants tells me.

The trip is not uncomfortable. There's space for us to lie down on top of the blankets and household items. My tenant companions say that from here to the north there is no need to fear *La Migra*. The first time the *Migra* placed roadblocks on this highway, at this time of the year, they say, was the last time. The *Migra* caught most of the wets who were headed north for the cherry harvest. The harvest rotted and the orchard owners complained and, ever since, they tell me, wets have been able to work in peace in Oregon.

Among those in the van are two peasants from Mr. Zavala's home town. Both are about forty years old. One is short and thin, and the other, even shorter but muscled, with short, thick arms,

191

a round face and protruding cheekbones. His mouth is wide, his lips are thick, his nose is short, and his eyeballs are yellowish. His voice is so harsh that it seems that he's speaking from inside a muffler. The others call him "Mr. Bad," they say, because a *gringo* gave him that nickname in Ripon. His *paisanos* say that in his native village, while he was drunk one time he stabbed a man with a screwdriver.

Also with us is the guy who says that he's a schoolteacher, and who is known among his companions as a man who spends all of his salary on personal items and winds up borrowing money for food. He brings his radio cassette player with him, and he's wearing a new denim overall that, he tells us with pride, would have been impossible to buy in Mexico. He's also got a wristwatch and a set of boots for field work, both purchased since he came to the U.S. He says that he only has ten dollars, but that doesn't worry him, since we won't have to pay for the trip until our first payday.

"What are you going to eat meanwhile?" Miguel asks him. "Between now and payday, you'll have to eat."

"Just like the saying, 'A man who plans is worth two,'" he tells us, pronouncing his words with an affected elegance. "If I run out of money, I'll sell some of my things. That's no problem. And in the worst of cases, you guys are my *paisanos*. Would you refuse me a loan?"

"That depends," Miguel says. "If we don't buy things because we want to be sure of having groceries, how are we going to loan to someone who spends everything? Besides, you can't count on *my* money because before we left, I sent a money order to my family."

Miguel is displeased with the teacher because Miguel is the one to whom the teacher always runs for a loan.

Two others who always spend their earnings, but on beer, are a pair from Michoacán who are also traveling with us. After every workday, these guys start by drinking a family-sized bottle of beer, one for each, and then pass the rest of the evening with smaller cans and bottles. They are the type who have to think twice before buying a set of clothes and a pair of shoes, for fear of depriving themselves of beer. And when they do buy, they also look for the cheapest clothing—when they're not buying used clothes, anyway. But nothing in life seems to bother them. They seem happy to be earning enough to keep them in food, clothes and beer. No one has ever seem them in a bad mood, and they entertain us during the trip with all sorts of quips, stories and jokes.

One of them, who calls himself Chon, tells about a prior trip

to the United States. He and several others were headed towards
Chicago with a coyote as a guide, when bad luck brought them
near the nose of *La Migra*. The coyote, on seeing that he'd been
spotted, had gone running off towards some nearby mountains,
leaving behind the car in which the group was traveling. The others
ran behind the coyote. In a few minutes, *La Migra* had caught
the whole bunch, except for Chon, who had run towards some
mountains on the opposite side of the road. The *Migra* left with
its captives and, at first, Chon believed that he was free. To make
sure, he kept running. When he decided to stop, he realized that he
did not know in what direction he was headed. It was wintertime
and snow had begun to fall. For a couple of days, he wandered
about in the wilds, without eating or sleeping, suffering from the
cold. On those nights he heard the howling of coyotes in the hills.
He wanted to find someone or be found, even if by the *Migra*, and
two or three times he yelled as loudly as he could. But his cries
were lost in the mountains. Finally, he came upon a dirt road and
he followed it to a ranch where people gave him aid. After telling
this story, Chon and his buddy, who took themselves to be true
men of worldly experience, watch our reactions, as if they regard
us as chickens who haven't yet left the egg.

Both of the two beer-guzzlers always look disheveled. Both
are short, and one of them is a little bit fat. They say that they
are Tarascan Indians. The schoolteacher has given the fat one the
nickname "Nopaltzín," after an Indian character in a comic book.
Nopaltzín has straight black hair that looks as if it had never known
a comb, and if he tried to use one, I doubt his hair would obey,
because it is thick and grows straight out, at a ninety-degree angle
from his skull. He wears a striped t-shirt that isn't big enough
to cover his paunch, leaving his navel showing. He can neither
read nor write. He speaks Spanish fluently, but like me, with the
accent of someone whose native language is an indigenous tongue.
This isn't the first time that he and Chon have gone to Oregon for
harvest. They tell us that to pick with speed, you've got to stick
the end of the branches under your arm, so that you can use both
hands to strip them of their fruit. They also tell us a couple of their
tricks. First, they say, you've got to toss leaves into your bucket,
along with fruits, and then, from time to time, you've got to agitate
the bucket, as if you were winnowing grain. That way, its contents
do not settle and the bucket looks full, when it isn't.

Northern California, with all its pine forests, reminds me of my
own region, where the pines sway in the breeze and the ground is
covered with dried needles, where the air is fresh and the sun, com-

forting. We stop several times during the trip to buy soft drinks or to eat at the parks that are along every road. We spend about four hours beside a river near Portland, watching a medium-sized ship pass through a type of canal in which the boat enters a compound, the water inside begins to decline and, after a while, the boat comes to rest on a dry cement floor. People unload the boat and then the compound or tank fills with water, little by little, until the boat is again floating. Then it leaves the compound and moves down the river.

After more than a day of travel, we come to a town in the state of Oregon, close to the border of the state of Washington. There are no mountains there, only hills. At places you can see them undulate in the distance, covered with thin vegetation. From that perspective, the terrain looks like the surface of a wind-blown lake. The town is a small one, whose six paved streets divide it into quadrants. Everything is quiet; few pedestrians or vehicles pass by. The town's houses are all made of wood, some more luxurious than others, and none of them as deteriorated as those I've seen in the Hispanic neighborhoods of big cities. The biggest building in town is its church, which is made of red brick. I don't see any Latins, except for the wetbacks who come and go in groups to the stores that occupy two blocks of the town's main street. The funny thing is, I don't recognize the faces of most of the wetbacks I see. When I comment about that to Nopaltzín, he tells me that ours is not the only group in town.

As soon as we arrive, the Zavala family rents a furnished apartment with kitchen and bath for sixty dollars a week. The man in denim who drove our van tells us that if we want, we, too, can form groups to rent apartments. We look around at each other, but nobody takes the initiative. By our silence, I take it that each of us feels somewhat uncomfortable with the others. At any rate, nobody is likely to want to room with the teacher, because of his habit of sponging, and the same goes for the two Tarascans. The driver tells us that if we don't want an apartment, that about ten minutes out of town there's a camp where we can live during the harvest without paying anything. But he warns us that it doesn't have any conveniences. All of us decide to stay there anyway.

THE CAMP

The camp is located by a cherry grove that, like the others I've seen, is planted in perfectly straight rows, despite the rises and falls of the terrain. There are two shacks, about 12' by 20' each, with dirt floors. The walls are of unpainted wood, and the roof is of sheet steel. A few yards away from the two shacks is a small concrete building with showers and commodes.

Inside the shacks are some old mattresses and some tarps that were originally used as tents, all of them dirty. Some of the guys pull the mattresses outside and hang them in the sun; later, they beat them with sticks, creating veritable clouds of dust.

"Hey, buddy! You'd better find yourself a mattress, or you'll have to sleep on the ground," one of them calls to me when he sees me taking life easy, looking at the fruit-laden trees.

I go into the shack and, not seeing any mattresses, I pull one out of the tarps to dust it in the yard. There are no brooms, but with some branches, we sweep the floors of the shacks until they are presentably clean. Then we prepare what will be our beds during the season. There are plenty of boards at hand, with which we make platforms for our mattresses and tarps.

Because the camp has been used for years, we also find kitchen utensils, rusting and dirty, but still serviceable. For a stove there's a steel drum or barrel outside, at whose base a hole has been cut and a grill inserted for holding firewood. Its top serves as a frying surface, like a *comal*.

By late afternoon, we have everything ready. All that's lacking is food to cook. We've divided ourselves into little groups, and I've fallen in with the two peasants from Puebla. Though all of us will use the same cooking equipment, the two Tarascans have set up a camp of their own in a tent they pitch in the yard. The problem of pooling money arises. The teacher offers only a dollar of the ten he had at the start of the trip. Miguel contributes his share, and Mr. Bad and I are also not without money.

"Now our problems are going to begin," Miguel says to the

teacher. "I wonder when the hour will come when you offer your radio for sale. Nobody has worked yet, so how can anybody buy it?"

"You're entirely right, *paisano*," the teacher tells him. "But I'll tell you what, I've got an idea to propose. Why don't you guys buy the food, and divide its cost between the four of you. I'll be left owing you my share, but in the meantime, I'll take care of the cooking. What do you think?"

"Well, that's not such a bad idea," Mr. Bad says, "on the condition that you pay us as soon as you get your first pay. And let's name somebody"—he points over towards me—"to keep track of the expenses in a notebook."

Everyone agrees.

Later on, a second group of wets arrive and take over one of the shacks. Several of them also pitch tents out in the yard.

We go to a little grocery store and buy eggs, two pounds of beans, a can of chiles in vinegar, flour tortillas and a jar of instant coffee.

"If we have to work tomorrow, I'll make the tacos," the teacher says.

For tacos to take to the field, we need aluminum foil, and I'm appointed to go buy it. When I come back, the others tell me that while I was gone, the driver of the van came to the camp with bad news. Too many pickers have arrived, he said, and this year we won't be paid two dollars and fifty cents a bucket, like last year, but only half as much. He told them that some 25,000 pickers had come to town. The men are discussing the news.

"The law of supply and demand," the teacher says. "If it was the opposite, not many workers and a lot of work, the pay would go up."

"Well, we can't go back," says Miguel, resignedly. "We're here and, unless something else comes up, we'll have to work at that rate."

We can't find a coffee pot, but the teacher digs in the trash around the camp until he finds a big can that once contained chiles. After washing it with water and sand, he makes two holes in its ends and passes a wire through them. Then he builds a fire and hangs the can over it. A little later water is boiling.

"A man ought to know how to survive with whatever he finds in reach," he says, proudly surveying his accomplishment.

The following day is an idle one. Nopaltzín suggests that we go into town. A bunch of us takes off walking with him.

"There's lots of wetbacks here, and what can we do? We all have a right to earn our daily bread," Nopaltzín remarks.

Upon crossing a street, we see a couple of white women who look at us curiously and say, "Hi!" When they've gone down the street a ways, Mr. Bad turns to watch them, rubbing his hands together as if he wants to follow them.

"What big blondes!" he exclaims.

"Don't fool yourself, Mr. Bad," Nopaltzín tells him. "They are ugly and even more than ugly, they're tall."

"So what were ladders invented for?" Mr. Bad answers.

"Content yourself with merely looking," Nopaltzín warns him. "Don't be ambitious. None of those blondes is for you."

"We can't complain. In Ripon we got them for twenty dollars," Miguel says. "The only thing is, these here aren't the same kind of women as those in Ripon were."

That afternoon, the driver in denim comes to the camp to tell us that he'll come by to take us to work at five in the morning.

"Bring tacos for the day. I don't want any of you falling out of the trees on me," he says.

PICKING CHERRIES

At the appointed hour, the driver comes for us in a station wagon. All of us who had come to town in the van get inside. We drive into the orchard, if that's what you can call a place so big that we drive for half an hour up and down hills, seeing only trees dotted with points of red. Even though now I am accustomed to such things in the United States, I'm still surprised to see that cherries are a big business, employing thousands and thousands of wetbacks.

"Get ready," the man in denim tells me. I've learned that his nickname is "Cherokee," because in his denims, with his long hair and tall stature, he looks like the American Indians whom I will later meet working among us in the orchards. But between them and us, there's not much way of telling who is Indian and who is Mexican, except that when you talk to them in Spanish, they answer in English.

"When we get there, grab your ladders," the Cherokee continues. "Grab the aluminum ones because they're not as heavy. Don't forget to get a picking bucket, either," he says.

A minute or two after he says this, the station wagon stops by a stack of ladders, aluminum and wooden ones stacked all together. The ladders are A-frames. Everybody tries to grab an aluminum one, but not everyone succeeds. Like children after breaking a *piñata*, after getting our ladders we all run towards the buckets. Some of the buckets are made in semi- circular form, with wide straps for crossing one's back and attaching to one's front side, at the stomach. The others are just plain buckets. When everyone has his work implements, we follow behind the Cherokee, who points each man to a tree, warning us again not to leave any ripe fruit upon its branches.

The trees have been pruned and they're not very tall. By the time the sun has come out from behind the hills, everybody is working. Some whistle, others sing, and those who are old friends entertain themselves by trading insults. Some carry on whole conversations, talking from tree to tree.

"Why do you eat the fruit, you fool!" someone says.

"Try them, you animal! They're delicious," somebody responds.

"Well, good, I was telling myself that it would be a pleasure to see you flying down from your tree in a hurry to find a place to go with diarrhea. You idiot, the cherries are covered with insecticide. If you're going to eat them, at least wash them with spit first."

We can also hear the teacher's radio playing in the distance.

Nopaltzín places his ladder almost vertically against a tree. After a while he loses his balance, and the ladder falls backwards. Nopaltzín tries to hang onto a branch, but his effort is futile. "Ay, son of a whore!" we hear him shout as it cracks. As he grabs for another branch, the bucket with the fruit he's gathered falls to the ground, but to his good fortune, it falls into soft, plowed dirt, a couple of yards from where the ladder has hit; nothing is spilled. The guys working nearest him get down and run to his aid. They find him laying down with his arms crossed on his chest, but not badly bruised.

Every few minutes, gusts of wind come through the orchard, raising great whirlwinds of dust that leave us looking like breaded veal cutlets. At the end of the day, we get into the same station wagon that brought us in the morning. Everyone asks everyone else how many buckets he filled. I filled nineteen, but one of the Tarascans, who has a lot of experience, filled twenty-five. The Cherokee tells us that the Zavala couple filled fifty-five. "That's experience for you," one of the Tarascans says.

Though we return to camp pretty dirty, the water that comes from the hose there is so cold that you can't stay under it for more than ten seconds without your body turning numb. Since we don't have a hot water heater, after one shower most of us decide that it's preferable to stay dirty during the whole work week.

The next day another one of us loses his balance and falls to the ground amidst the laughter of those who see him. Among the voices is that of Nopaltzín. "Ah, but how dumb you are! You haven't learned that to go up and down one uses a ladder," he chides.

After a week's work, the Cherokee brings us our paychecks. Each one of us has kept his own count of the buckets he's picked, and we compare these tallies with the paychecks. We don't find any fraud. After cashing our paychecks at the little grocery store— which doesn't charge us anything for cashing them—we settle accounts with the teacher, "before he can go to town to invest his paycheck," Miguel says.

After Miguel complains that he is tired of eating only tacos of eggs and beans, we agree to buy a few pounds of meat that we take to cook on our improvised stove. The Tarascans cooperate with us, only they pay their share by buying beer.

The weeks pass by. Every morning at five the car comes for us and about every four or five days, takes us to a new part of the orchard. We get paid every Saturday morning. We spend our weekends drinking, or playing cards, or walking downtown. The teacher continues "saving" money in his own peculiar way, only now, he is current in his share of the grocery bill.

A SUNDAY

One Sunday morning, two neatly-dressed, white-skinned preachers come to the camp, accompanied by a young woman with silken blonde hair and a sharp-featured face. All three come in a recent-model car. They smile and pass out brochures to those who crowd around. The preachers speak in Spanish, and listeners form a circle around them. The young woman stays in the car, moving her blue eyes this way and that. A lot of men give her looks, because it's not common to see a woman of such fine features in the middle of the dirt, trees and old shacks whose inhabitants smell of sweat and grime.

Nopaltzín and his friend are sitting on the ground, each one with his can of beer. His friend points towards the visitors, but Nopaltzín makes gestures of indifference. He takes a swig of his can of beer and holds the can to his lips until it is empty, then reaches out for his friend to pass him another from the case at his side. He crushes the empty can in his fist and throws it at the electric light post, but misses.

"Look how these *bolillos* have us," he says, nodding towards the preachers.

"They are preachers," Nopaltzín says with a shrug. "Ugh! Like these, I run into thousands and I know what they talk about."

The door of the car opens and at last the young blonde gets out. She is of ordinary height and is thin. Her cotton dress is pink and it covers her to her calves. Just like her face, her movements are delicate, but her high heels don't allow her to walk with ease over the rocky ground. Like her companions, she smiles at everyone, only when she smiles, we notice her perfect white teeth.

"Just look at that!" Nopaltzín exclaims on seeing her. "Just look at what God has sent us! For a beautiful woman like that, even I am willing to listen to the Word."

His friend breaks out laughing after looking at the girl and at Nopaltzín, who is headed towards the circle.

"Just what are you laughing at, you big animal?" Nopaltzín

201

asks him.

"I don't have a mirror, but if I did, I'd show it to you so that you could see yourself," his friend replies.

"I just want to say hello to her. What's wrong with that?" Nopaltzín asks.

"She doesn't speak Spanish," his friend says.

"Well, I've got to say hello. If she doesn't speak Spanish, I'll speak English."

Then we see Nopaltzín walk towards her. He smiles at her in a frank and haughty way, and speaks in the manner of one who is sure of what he is saying.

"Talk to me," he says in English. "I want to hear you preach," he says in Spanish. And with his finger he points to the sky.

The blonde blushes, then smiles at Nopaltzín in an apologetic way, pointing at her companions so that Nopaltzín will join the group. But Nopaltzín shakes his head, no. He makes signs, pointing first to her, then to himself. Then he puts both palms together at chest level, so as to say, "Nopaltzín dead." Then he points to the sky.

The girl must have understood because she invites him to come close to the group, but he makes signs indicating that he wants to hear from her, not from them. The girl shrugs and says, "I'm sorry."

Nopaltzín backs off, but before going he says to her in English, "You are beautiful."

She tells him thanks.

THE WOMEN IN THE BAR

One Saturday afternoon in the camp, while drinking some beers with Miguel, we decide to go look for a bar in town, because it's not the same to be drinking beer on the bare ground as to be drinking at a comfortable table, listening to music and having the possibility of meeting some women. After walking a few times down the town's few streets, we notice a bar called Farmers' Bar. As I try to go inside, the bartender stops me, demanding to see my identification, because, he says, I don't look like a man of drinking age. I show him the same card I showed the police in Los Angeles. The bar is a small place, with only four tables, with four chairs at each. Most of the clientele is white. We sit down at the bar and then notice that in a corner of the place are two white women more than thirty years old. They're the only women in the bar and they're in the company of a couple of wetbacks.

"They beat us to them," Miguel comments.

"Well, if it's that way, it doesn't matter," someone else says.

Half an hour later the wets who are sitting with the women get up from their chairs and leave the bar.

"Come on, buddy!" Miguel demands of me. "Let's go where they are."

Miguel trusts that I speak English, because whenever they've had to go to the store, I've been the one who has talked to the storekeepers, asking for this or that. But the truth is, my English isn't enough to sustain a conversation.

"Well, let's just say hello, because I don't speak much English," I tell him.

"It's no big deal. I know that you can, and if you can't, we'll leave like those guys just did."

We go up to the women, who are now talking to each other.

"Hi!" I say.

"Do you speak English?" one of them asks immediately, and I realize that the other wets must have left because they ran out of conversation.

203

"A little," I say.

"Well, sit down," she invites us.

"Nobody speak Spanish?" I ask, knowing that they don't, but knowing, as well, that I've got to say something.

"No, I don't," one of them answers.

"This is my friend, Miguel," I say. "Michael, in English."

"Yes, Miguel, Michael," they say, entertained.

Then I tell Miguel to shake hands with them. Then I introduce myself and they ask how to say my name in English. I know, but to prolong things, I write my name on a paper napkin and ask them how to pronounce it.

"*¿Qué están tomando?*" Miguel says to them.

"What is he saying?" they ask me.

"What are you drinking?" I explain.

"Oh, Margaritas!" they say.

Miguel turns towards the bartender and with signs he tells him to serve another round to the women and to us.

We sit and talk to them in this way for hours, me scratching my head to recall the English words that I learned in school. They tell us their names in English, but the truth is, I only pretend to understand, because I can't pronounce what I hear. When they ask where I come from, I tell them that I come from the state of Oaxaca, and just like the Chicanos in San Antonio, they admiringly repeat, "Oaxaca! Oaxaca!" They, too, ask me about the magic mushrooms of María Sabinas. "The Shaman," they say she is called. I lie. I tell them that I am from the same town and that I eat the mushrooms regularly.

We pay for the Margaritas and more beer, the glasses are emptied and we pay for more beers and Margaritas. All the while they speak words that we struggle to understand. Miguel, who has kept silent, all of sudden tells them that they are very pretty, and they ask me to translate what he has said. Finally, the bartender says that he doesn't want to sell us any more drinks. As we are leaving, each one of them gives us a kiss that tastes of Margaritas, and I ask if they are going to abandon us to the cold.

They look at each other and laugh, and then the tall, thin one says, "Get in," pointing towards her car. By this hour of the night, the town is deserted. The car heads out of town, towards where the orchards begin. Only the trees know what happened next.

Two hours later, Miguel and I are walking towards the camp. He can't stop thanking me. The sun hasn't yet come up when we arrive, and our companions are still asleep. Miguel wakes them with whistles and shouts of joy. The guys get out of their beds and ask what happened.

"We got a hold of some white girls! But what girls they were! You can't imagine it!" Then Miguel tells them everything, moving his hands like he still had the women in his arms.

"Ah, how did you do it, if you don't speak English," the teacher says, incredulously.

"What do you mean, we don't speak English? I don't, but my buddy here does! I don't know what he was telling them, but it's a fact that it worked." While he brags, Miguel is whistling and shouting as if he were herding cattle.

"Is that true, buddy?" the professor asks me, not wanting to credit Miguel's story.

"Sure it's true."

"Do you speak English?" he persists.

"Not much, but it was enough."

"I'll buy the beers tomorrow!" the professor says. "You can get women for the rest of us."

"I'll pay the beers, too," Mr. Bad says. "You don't have to do anything but talk English."

The next day, we all go to the bar, but we don't have the same luck.

THE CHINESE RESTAURANT

Because so many workers come, most weeks we work only three days, and our earnings are not great, because most of the time, they take us to pick over trees whose fruits were green on the first picking. The Zavala family begins making plans to return to Ripon. The teacher says that he is going to New York, where his parents are living. In order to finance the trip, he puts up for sale his watch, his cassette player, a fourteen-carat gold chain and a jean jacket. Cherokee comes to the camp to offer jobs to two men needed by a ranch to maintain its orchard; the two Tarascans take the offer. Miguel and Mr. Bad propose that I join them in buying a car to go to the state of Washington, where they say a harvest of oranges is nearing. They figure that my English will help them find a job, and they know that I can drive, too. But after we've made our plans, the man who owns the car that they want to buy tells us that the car isn't in good enough condition to make long trips. We look for another car to buy, but don't come up with anything. There's nothing for us to do but return to Ripon with the Zavalas.

When we return, the Zavala family asks the contractors with which it deals when work will be available for us. They learn that the plum harvest is due in about two weeks. But a few days afterwards, I become bored of waiting, and I buy a ticket back to Los Angeles. People in the Zavala family tell me to be patient, that work is on its way. I tell them thanks, but I leave, anyway. Miguel and Mr. Bad ask me to take them with me, if I have a sure chance of a job, but I have to tell them that I don't know what kind of luck awaits me.

On arriving at my uncle's house, I find that five men are already living there. The owner, after seeing me come and go for several days, tells my uncle that he didn't intend for that many men to occupy the place, and he threatens to raise the rent. I make a few telephone calls, explaining my situation, and villager Rolando offers me quarters in his apartment.

Rolando is thirty-three, and he works as a busboy in a Chinese restaurant. His wife, two years younger than he, works as a maid, cleaning houses. They give me a place to stay on the condition that I help to pay the rent. The apartment, which costs them three hundred and ninety dollars a month, is furnished, with air conditioning and new carpeting on the floor.

For the next two months I go around without work, repeating the same routine as before, from business to business. In response to several ads, I fill out several applications for jobs through a Spanish-language newspaper. But during these two months, I earn only seven dollars. I go to visit Rafael, another of the townsmen who has a job at four dollars an hour, delivering tortillas to Mexican restaurants in his own car. The day I visit, Rafael has already finished his route, and at its end, several plastic packages, each containing packets of three dozen tortillas, are left over. He proposes that we go door-to-door in a Mexican neighborhood until we sell them. We each take a box of tortillas and go into peoples' yards and up the steps of apartment buildings, hawking our ware. After the first few sales, we hit upon the idea of establishing ourselves as door-to-door tortilla sales and delivery men. The idea seems like a good one, since Rafael already owns a car. But we abandon the thought when our customers tell us that they are already served by a tortilla vendor. Nevertheless, we sell more than thirty packets.

It comes as a surprise to me when Rolando and his wife, Cristina, decide to make a trip home. Rolando leaves me his job as a busboy. Because they're required for the job, I buy myself a pair of black pants, a couple of white shirts and a black sport coat. Rolando leaves me the apartment and some of his possessions, including a bicycle, which he has used for riding to work and an old car, similar to the one I had in San Antonio. He also leaves me part of the next month's rent payment, saying that if all goes as planned, he'll be back within four or five weeks. A day before he quits, I go to the restaurant with him for an interview with its owner.

The restaurant is located in a one-story, red brick building, with bamboo plants in the flowerbeds outside. On one side of the building sits a paved parking lot with space for thirty cars. The interior of the place is carpeted in red, and there are tables to seat about fifty people. The walls are painted yellow, and are hung with paintings of oriental scenes. Plastic lanterns, also decorated with Asian scenes, hang from the ceiling.

In one corner of the kitchen, high up on the wall, the image of Buddha sits on an altar between a couple of porcelain vases filled with plastic flowers. The altar is lighted with a single red bulb that is mounted inside a plastic facsimile candle, which is itself mounted in a plastic facsimile candelabra. Upon the altar, as an offering someone has placed a tiny porcelain cup of tea, three apples and a wooden incense burner. While we are waiting for the owner to arrive, Rolando shows me the routine that will be mine.

The owner arrives in a bright-colored Mercedes Benz. Rolando and I are outside when he pulls up. He is about forty- five years old, of medium height, dressed in a gray suit. On getting out of his car, he walks towards us and then stops, crossing his arms and staring at us in silence. Sometimes he blinks, and when he does, I note that his eyelids are swollen.

"So you are cleaning up, eh?" he says to Rolando at last. "Don't forget to water the plants."

Then he goes inside the restaurant. Rolando decides that he'd better water the plants, and after he does that, we go inside ourselves.

On a wall of the anteroom that leads to the owner's office is a time clock and, next to it, a rack where time cards are stored. Not far away hangs a framed copy of a restaurant review from the *Los Angeles Times*. The office itself is small, with only enough space for the boss' desk and a couple of file cabinets. Cardboard boxes sit on each side of the two file cabinets. Rolando and I stand in the entryway. The boss' back is turned towards us.

"Excuse me," Rolando says to announce our presence.

"Ah!" we hear the owner exclaim. He is leafing through some printed pages, and he seems to be absorbed. "What do you want?" he asks without turning around.

"This is the guy who is going to work in my place," Rolando says.

The owner swivels in his chair, facing us. He looks at me with a grimace of surprise, and I see him close his eyelids even further. He looks like someone who is trying to overcome a hangover. Then, without saying a word to me, he directs himself to Rolando.

"When are you leaving?"

"Next week, but today is my last workday, because it's the end of the pay period."

"When will you be back?"

"In three months."

"Well, when you get back, let me know immediately," the owner tells him.

"But he'll be working here," Rolando says, pointing to me.

"That doesn't matter. The job is yours, anyway."

The owner puts both hands over his mouth while he yawns. He plays with the knot of his tie. He swivels back towards his desk and begins leafing through papers again.

"Does he speak English?" he says, as if in afterthought.

"Ask him," Rolando says.

"Not too much, sir, but I understand what you say," I tell him. Rolando has already explained to me that it isn't necessary to speak much English, and that what one needs to know can be learned on the job.

The owner continues leafing through his documents, as if he were completely entertained. We begin to think that he has forgotten our presence.

"That's all right," he says after a few minutes of silence. "Let him prove that he can work."

I am one of fourteen employees of the restaurant. There are six waitresses, uniformed in black dresses and golden blouses with oriental adornments. There's a middle-aged doorman, who wears black pants and a white shirt. The cooks wear street clothing, but cover themselves with white cotton aprons. The dishwasher wears a plastic apron, to protect against getting wet. Only the dishwasher and I are Mexican. The rest of the employees are Orientals.

Being a busboy isn't, in my view, the most pleasant calling in the world. I had wanted to find a job in a furniture shop, as in San Antonio, so that I might pick up skills to use in my family's shop at home. But nevertheless, being a busboy represents a step upward, because the lowest rung of status is that of dishwasher. The working conditions are enviable, and I consider myself lucky to have a job. My working hours at the restaurant are from eleven in the morning until eleven at night, six days a week. My salary is six hundred dollars a month, paid every fifteen days, plus the tips that make my job better than a dishwasher's.

The owner's wife, who calls herself Ana, is about forty years old. She is short and so thin that her face looks like skin stretched over a skull. Her lips are formless, making her mouth seem like nothing more than a hole. She has a small nose, and her eyes, buried back inside the cover of her head, seem to be peering out at everything. She walks with a hurried step, her feet seeming to kick things in front of her. When Rolando introduces me, she stops moving for a short instant, sweeps my face with a stare, and makes an unintelligible, little whine. Then, as if an emergency had arisen, she gives me an order. "Clean! Clean!" she says, moving her bony right hand in a waving motion, signaling the whole restaurant.

"She's a slave driver," Rolando says to me. "If you have any problems, go to the owner, not to her."

During my first days on the job, I have trouble with the language, but I conclude that English can't be learned all at once. In a carpentry shop, I wouldn't have much trouble understanding instructions about measurements, tools and woods. The same in a print shop, or in a car wash, because even though I've always worked with Chicanos, they speak a mixture of English and Spanish, as when they say, "*púchalo*" for push, "*trínelo*" for "train him," "*trustear*" for trust, "*carrucha*" for car, "*scrapes*" for scraps, and lots of other things whose origins are in English. But now, working in a restaurant, I find that I don't know the basic vocabulary. For example, if a diner asks me to bring him the pepper, I understand perfectly when he says "Bring me the . . . ," but his last word leaves me blank. A few customers ask me questions about the dishes we serve, and when they do, my confusion is double, because the items on our menu all have Chinese names. Other patrons throw out long phrases and then stare at me, waiting for my answer, only to hear me tell them, "I'm sorry, sir, I don't understand you." They shake their heads and then stretch their necks, looking for a waitress.

Sometimes the clients resort to hand signals, saving me from jams. To ask for a napkin, they'll pretend to be wiping their faces. A few others, wanting to be friendly, try to speak Spanish.

THE WORKDAY

My tasks are simple, as they were at the car wash. I come and go from the kitchen to the dining room. To make myself known as a good busboy, I have to agilely remove dirty plates and tablecloths, taking everything to the dishwasher's table in one trip to the kitchen, without dropping anything. Then I have to return to the dining room with a tablecloth, napkins and the place settings. With only two motions, I have to lay out the table cloth so that it falls perfectly over the table, and place the silverware on the table with speed and dexterity, like a professional player, dealing cards.

During moments when there are no tables to clean, I get my plastic pitcher of ice water and refill the empty glasses on customers' tables, or with my metal pitcher, refill cups of hot tea. I continually encounter capricious clients. Their tea is cold and they want it changed for hot tea. Or it's too hot, and they want a cube of ice to chill it. Or it's too weak, or too strong. Bring me sauce, or more salt, or pepper, or a fork, or a knife, or more rice. Orders come at me from all directions and it's my job to fulfill them speedily, smiling courteously, as if I were happy to be serving.

When the restaurant is full, everything becomes a mixture of disorderly sound. Coughing, the constant ting-ting of the forks on the plates, small laughs, feminine shrieks, and never-ending conversations. In the kitchen, everything is a confusion of shouts. The waitresses shout to order this plate or that, the cooks announce the dishes that are ready, and the meat hisses when it comes it contact with the boiling oil of the frying pans. In one corner the dishwasher stands with a mountain of plates at his side, one by one washing the food remains away with a hose that shoots pressurized water. He places them on a plastic rack before putting them into the dishwashing machine. In order to keep from being buried by the arriving plates, he, too, has to be agile, like a juggler. You can hear the Chinese cooks shouting, "¡Amigo! Plates!" The dishwasher responds with an insult, raising his right hand and shooting them the finger.

211

Every morning the Buddha image is an object of reverence. The owner's wife lights a stick of incense and puts it in the little wooden bowl that stands in front of the idol. Then she clasps her hands in front of her, at forehead height, and bows before it three times, murmuring between her lips.

One afternoon, when business is lax, one of the waitresses walks up and down in the empty dining room with her arms crossed behind her back. Every now and then she says, "No money!" opening her arms and showing me empty hands.

"I know why," I tell her, trying to adopt a serious tone.

"You know why and don't say anything?" she says, irritated.

"It's simple," I say in the same tone. "The Buddha needs a dollar."

I heard her cursing and complaining for a little longer, but then, all of a sudden, she goes to her purse and takes out a dollar. She takes the dollar to the kitchen, places it in front of the Buddha, clasps her hands, bows and mutters.

But only a half dozen clients come that afternoon.

THE FENDER-BENDER

One night after work, I drive Rolando's old car to visit some friends, and then head towards home. At a light, I come to a stop too late, leaving the front end of the car poking into the crosswalk. I shift into reverse, but as I am backing up, I strike the van behind me. Its driver immediately gets out to inspect the damage to his vehicle. He's a tall Anglo-Saxon, dressed in a deep blue work uniform. After looking at his car, he walks up to the window of the car I'm driving.

"Your drivers license," he says, a little enraged.

"I didn't bring it," I tell him.

He scratches his head. He is breathing heavily with fury.

"Okay," he says. "You park up ahead while I call a patrolman."

The idea of calling the police doesn't sound good to me, but the accident is my fault. So I drive around the corner and park at the curb. I turn off the motor and hit the steering wheel with one fist. I don't have a drivers' license. I've never applied for one. Nor do I have with me the identification card that I bought in San Antonio. Without immigration papers, without a driving permit, and having hit another car, I feel as if I'm just one step away from Mexico.

I get out of the car. The white man comes over and stands right in front of me. He's almost two feet taller.

"If you're going to drive, why don't you carry your license?" he asks in an accusatory tone.

"I didn't bring it," I say, for lack of any other defense.

I look at the damage to his car. It's minor, only a scratch on the paint and a pimple-sized dent.

"I'm sorry," I say. "Tell me how much it will cost to fix, and I'll pay for it, that's no problem." I'm talking to him in English, and he seems to understand.

"This car isn't mine," he says. "It belongs to the company I work for. I'm sorry, but I've got to report this to the police, so that I don't have to pay for the damage."

"That's no problem," I tell him again. "I can pay for it."

After we've exchanged these words, he seems less irritated. But he says he'd prefer for the police to come, so that they can report that the dent wasn't his fault.

While we wait, he walks from one side to the other, looking down the avenue this way and that, hoping that the police will appear.

Then he goes over to the van to look at the dent.

"It's not much," he says. "If it was my car, there wouldn't be any problems, and you could go on."

After a few minutes, the long-awaited police car arrives. Only one officer is inside. He's a Chicano, short and of medium complexion, with short, curly hair. On getting out of the car, he walks straight towards the Anglo.

The two exchange a few words.

"Is that him?" he asks, pointing at me.

The Anglo nods his head.

Speaking in English, the policeman orders me to stand in front of the car and to put my hands on the hood. He searches me and finds only the car keys and my billfold with a few dollars in it. He asks for my drivers license.

"I don't have it," I answer in Spanish.

He wrinkles his face into a frown, and casting a glance at the Anglo, shakes his head in disapproval of me.

"That's the way these Mexicans are," he says.

He turns back towards me, asking for identification. I tell him I don't have that, either.

"You're an illegal, eh?" he says.

I won't answer.

"An illegal," he says to himself.

"Where do you live?" he continues. He's still speaking in English.

I tell him my address.

"Do you have anything with you to prove that you live at that address?" he asks.

I think for a minute, then realize that in the glove compartment is a letter that my parents sent to me several weeks earlier.

I show him the envelope and he immediately begins to write something in a little book that he carries in his back pocket. He walks to the back of my car and copies the license plate number. Then he goes over to his car and talks into his radio. After he talks, someone answers. Then he asks me for the name of the car's owner.

He goes over to where the Anglo is standing. I can't quite hear what they're saying. But when the two of them go over to look at the dent in the van, I hear the cop tell the Anglo that if he wants, he can file charges against me. The Anglo shakes his head and explains what he had earlier explained to me, about only needing for the police to certify that he wasn't responsible for the accident. The Anglo says that he doesn't want to accuse me of anything because the damage is light.

"If you want, I can take him to jail," the cop insists.

The Anglo turns him down again.

"If you'd rather, we can report him to Immigration," the cop continues.

Just as at the first, I am now almost sure that I'll be making a forced trip to Tijuana. I find myself searching my memory for my uncle's telephone number, and to my relief, I remember it. I am waiting for the Anglo to say yes, confirming my expectations of the trip. But instead, he says no, and though I remain silent, I feel appreciation for him. I ask myself why the Chicano is determined to harm me. I didn't really expect him to favor me, just because we're of the same ancestry, but on the other hand, once I had admitted my guilt, I expected him to treat me at least fairly. But even against the white man's wishes, he's trying to make matters worse for me. I've known several Chicanos with whom, joking around, I've reminded them that their roots are in Mexico. But very few of them see it that way. Several have told me how when they were children, their parents would take them to vacation in different states of Mexico, but their own feeling, they've said, is, "I am an American citizen!" Finally, the Anglo, with the justifying paper in his hands, says goodbye to the cop, thanks him for his services, gets into his van and drives away.

The cop stands in the street in a pensive mood. I imagine that he's trying to think of a way to punish me.

"Put the key in the ignition," he orders me.

I do as he says.

Then he orders me to roll up the windows and lock the doors.

"Now, go on, walking," he says.

I go off, taking slow steps. The cops gets in his patrol car and stays there, waiting. I turn the corner after two blocks and look out for my car, but the cops is still parked beside it. I begin looking for a coat hanger, and after a good while, find one by a curb of the street. I keep walking, keeping about two blocks away from the car. While I walk, I bend the coat hanger into the form I'll need. As if I'd called for it, a speeding car goes past. When it comes to the avenue where my car is parked, it makes a turn. It is going so fast that its wheels screech as it rounds the corner. The cop turns on the blinking lights of his patrol car and leaving black marks on the pavement beneath it, shoots out to chase the speeder. I go up to my car and with my palms force a window open a crack. Then I insert the clothes hanger in the crack and raise the lock lever. It's a simple task, one that I'd already performed. This wasn't the first time that I'd been locked out of a car, though always before, it was because I'd forgotten to remove my keys.

THE NEW YEAR

The owner lets us eat at the restaurant three times a day, without discounting our meals from our salaries, but the food we're allowed isn't anything to get excited about. It is much better at the close of business on Chinese New Year's Day. Then, instead of macaroni soup, bits of grease and the joints of chicken bones, we are given fried fish and a bottle of beer of an oriental brand, courtesy of the restaurant. On top of that, we're allowed to eat on the dining room tables. After that, the owner gives each one of us a present. It is an envelope decorated with golden drawings.

"This is for good luck!" he says on handing us our envelopes. "Happy New Year!"

Inside the envelope, I find two dollars.

FEARS OF *LA MIGRA*

One night, the Spanish-language television channel sounds the alarm. *La Migra*, its reporter says, has begun casting nets in downtown Los Angeles and everywhere wetbacks are presumed to circulate. An announcer advises us not to leave our houses unnecessarily, not to wait too long at bus stops, and if possible, to catch rides to work. On the television screen are filmed images of detentions. An anchorman emphasizes the same message on the following day, but the broadcast also reports that the streets are deserted, and that businessmen are complaining about falling sales. In a lot of work places, wetbacks don't show up as usual. I keep going to work, and when it comes time to return at night, the waitresses offer to take me home. I don't refuse their offers. But the panic over the *Migra* only lasts a couple of days, and after that, everything returns to normal.

TRANSLATIONS

I am useful at the restaurant as more than a busboy. All the time, I have to intervene when the owner wants to communicate something to Fabian, the dish washer. Once, for example, Fabian is bending over a plastic pail, washing the towels that are used to clean tables in the dining room. Passing by, the owner looks over. He stops to watch. Then, as is his custom, he furrows his brow to show his displeasure.

"*Amigo*," he says, trying to speak Spanish. "*¿No comer?*"

Fabian raises his head and looks disconcertedly at the owner, while the owner repeats his question.

"What does this son-of-a-bitch want?" Fabian calls to me in Spanish.

"He's asking if you haven't eaten," I tell him.

Fabian reacts like someone has discovered that there's nothing to worry about, after all. He tells me that he's eaten a double ration, and so that the owner will understand, he rubs his stomach, indicating that he's full.

The owner, without changing his unpleasant expression, takes a couple of long steps, snaps up one of the towels and gives it four or five energetic blows against the inside of the pail, showing Fabian just how he wants him to work.

"*Ándale, así ... ¡No comer!*" he scolds.

Another time the owner leans into the kitchen just when the chief cook, an Oriental about forty years old, short, fat and pot-bellied, is heatedly arguing with Fabian. They are face-to-face, with only an inch in between them. Without catching their breaths, they insult one another, one speaking in Spanish, the other in Cantonese. Blood has rushed to their faces, turning both of them red. The cook grabs one of the plates by his side and with gestures threatens to throw it at Fabian. Fabian picks up a plate, too. Disgusted or afraid, the cook throws his plate onto the floor.

The owner, who has watched all this without saying a word, tells them both to come to his office. Soon, four of us are gathered there: the owner, Fabian, the cook and me. The cook complains of the disobedience of the dishwasher, who complains that the cook gives him too much work to do. I am the translator between Fabian and the owner, and the owner is the translator between the cook and me, because Fabian speaks only Spanish, and the cook, only Chinese. It takes all my effort to translate for Fabian and the boss, and the truth is, I do it more by deduction than from knowing English.

They make peace, but the other employees hassle Fabian more every day. The waitresses quit leaving him the little tip which they sometimes give, though it never comes to more than two dollars a day. The other cooks keep piling work onto him and keep complaining to the owner that he works too slowly.

Fabian comes to me one day, saying that he wants to talk to the owner about a raise, and also to complain about not receiving the tip from the waitresses. "Let me think about it," the owner tells him. A little later, the owner asks me if I have any friends or know anyone who wants to work as a dishwasher. I tell him that I don't know of anyone who needs a job, though, of course, I know several jobless wets; the problem is, I don't want to help the owner displace Fabian. Every day wets come to the restaurant door, looking for work, but the owner has a rule: he doesn't hire strangers. He's never hired anyone except people he already knows, or people whom other employees have introduced.

STRANGE BARS

At the end of a particularly hard day of work, Fabian suggests to me that "a cold beer would help kill our tiredness." We decide to go to a bar that is located down the street from the restaurant. I have brought my bicycle, which I chain to a post in front of the bar. But it takes us less time to open the door and enter than it does to leave. The place, we learn in a glance, isn't an ordinary bar.

Huge photographs of nude men hang on the wall above the bar. Beyond the bar are two rooms with screen wire walls, or mesh privacy screens, and in one of the rooms we see two men very close to one another. We turn to leave as soon as we've seen this, and as we go out, we ignore the voice of the bartender saying, "Can I help you with something?"

Still determined to drink a beer, we find another bar, about a block on the other side of the restaurant. From the street we can hear a juke box playing rock 'n roll.

"Let's go see if this place is decent," I say as I chain my bicycle to the nearest light post.

On entering, we see nothing unusual, except an absence of women. A dozen customers are around the bar, some sitting, others standing. The rest of the place is vacant. The tables and chairs are arranged in lines on each side of a little wooden wall, atop of which planters have been placed. In the dark light I can't determine if the plants in them are artificial or real. We sit down at the bar and order our beers. As we sip at them, we trade comments about the previous bar.

"That's just one of the many surprises the United States has for us," I tell Fabian.

We haven't finished even half of our beers when a customer comes in and sits down about four chairs from us. The bartender, a corpulent, bearded white man, is busy taking care of one of the customers at the other end of the bar. The newly arrived customer says something in the bartender's direction. The bartender looks his way, and then with hurried steps comes to the guy's barstool, nearly sitting on his lap. The newly arrived customer stretches his neck, puckers his lips like a trumpet player and kisses the bartender. For the same reason that we'd left the first bar, we drink the rest of our beers in a hurry, pay and go. We decide not to try any more bars. Instead, we go to the nearest convenience store, buy a six-pack and split it. I get onto my bicycle and Fabian goes to the bus stop. From now on, we'll drink our beers at home.

THE FIGHT

Five months pass before Rolando and Cristina return. Rolando tells me that he doesn't want to resume his job as busboy. Instead, he wants to look for a job as a helper in an auto body shop. But he stops by the restaurant, just to visit. The owner is so happy to see him that he slaps Rolando on the back.

"Good, how good it is that you're back. You've come to work?" he asks.

"I'm not sure," Rolando says.

"Why not?"

Rolando breaks into a smile, takes a deep breath and answers.

"I'll come back if you'll pay me seven hundred dollars a month and an increase in my share of the tip money."

"Tell me if you're coming to work," the owner says. "The raise, we'll take care of that in a couple of weeks."

"I'm not sure. Give me a week to think about."

"That's fine. When you're ready, just call me," the owner says.

Rolando was just trying his luck. He knows that the owner doesn't give in so easily. Rolando has been working for him for two and a half years, and he's only gotten one pay raise: for fifty dollars a month.

The conflicts between Fabian and the cook grow worse. One day when Fabian is mopping the floor, the edge of his mop passes over the foot of the chief cook, who is standing in the kitchen, peeling carrots. Fabian asks the cook to pardon him, but the cook thinks that Fabian mopped his foot on purpose. He lunges into Fabian, hitting him in the ribs, hard enough to knock him against the wall. The rest of the cooks laugh when they see Fabian doubled-over, holding his rib cage in pain. Suddenly, Fabian sticks the cook in the ribs, using the mop handle as his lance. Then the two begin to trade blows. They wrestle and knock each other around, bumping against walls and tables as they go. Their fight creates a racket. The waitresses come running and, from a corner of the kitchen, laugh at the scene. Three porcelain plates go crashing into the

223

floor, following a blow by one of the combatants. After a few more seconds, a narrow stream begins flowing from Fabian's nose, and the cook's lips and teeth are likewise bathed in blood, from a split opened in his upper lip. Another blow from the cook sends Fabian slumping onto the dish washing machine. The dishwasher fumbles around in the dirty plates and dishes, fishes out a knife, and leaps towards the cook, who skips away and keeps moving, apparently convinced that Fabian will turn him to slices. "I'm going to send you to the other world, you low-life Chinaman," Fabian yells.

The waitresses shriek when they see Fabian's butcher knife. The cook takes refuge behind a table, while the rest of the cooks press themselves against the wall, too scared to move. Then the owner steps in, brought by one of the waitresses.

"What's going on?" he shouts in English.

In an instant, everyone becomes quiet. Fabian puts his knife down on one of the tables, takes out a handkerchief from his pocket and wipes the blood from his nose. The cook wipes his mouth and spits blood between his teeth. The rest of the cooks break the silence, talking in Chinese and casting glances towards Fabian. The waitresses don't say anything. Fabian looks towards me, then tries to say something to the owner, hoping that I'll translate. But the boss doesn't want to hear anything. He orders Fabian to meet him outside. The boss goes to his office, then goes outside and hands Fabian his paycheck, telling him that he's been fired.

THE LABOR OFFICE

The restaurant is left without a dishwasher, so the owner tells me to take Fabian's place. That means that I won't be getting the tip that I had grown used to as a busboy, about five dollars a day. At the boss' request, I tell Rolando to show up for work, passing along the message that if he'll return, the boss promises to hear his pay request again within two weeks. Rolando comes back as busboy, and I stay on as dishwasher. Three weeks pass, and Rolando still hasn't received a raise. Though he has reminded the owner several times, the owner always asks for more time. Little by little, Rolando quits exerting himself, and begins losing the owner's confidence. After thirty days, the owner refuses to give Rolando a raise. Rolando quits.

"He's crazy," the boss says to me later. "He wants too much money."

The restaurant is again without a busboy. A Chicano is hired, and because he speaks English, he gets Rolando's place, not mine.

A few hours after he starts working, the Chicano comes into the kitchen, very much alarmed.

"Listen, *compañero*," he says, "what does the lousy boss think he's doing? Man, I saw him punch my timecard!"

He goes on to say that he pointed out to the owner that he wasn't supposed to punch employees' cards, and that the owner told him that with or without timecards, the busboy's salary was six hundred dollars a month.

"That's against the law!" the Chicano exclaims.

On his fourth day at work, the Chicano quits. Before leaving, he tells me that there's a government office where we can report the owner, file a claim and, if we win, collect back pay for the hours we've worked and haven't been paid. When I get home, I explain this to Rolando, who immediately calculates how much he could collect for the two and a half years he worked at the restaurant. We get in touch with the Chicano, who has left me his telephone number. Then the three of us go to present our complaint to the labor office. We decide that I will not sign my name, because I still need my job at the restaurant.

To my good fortune, the owner hires another wet, one who knows less English than I do. They give him the dish washer's job and I go back to being busboy. Rolando finds a job in another restaurant as a busboy, and months pass without us learning anything about the claim we filed at the labor office. Then one day when I show up at work, everybody seems to be in a dark mood. The owner's wife gives me an accusing look. The boss comes in with his head down, and I don't hear him say a word all day. From time to time the cooks gather together and talk, as if something surprising were afoot, and once, I hear them mention Rolando's name. The waitresses put on long faces when the owner is near, but in his absence, they chat gaily. My suspicions are confirmed when, at closing time, the owner asks me if I know where Rolando is, or when he went to the labor office.

I act as if I don't understand. I say that Rolando is still looking for a job, and that he goes to the employment office every day. A cloud of suspicion seems to leave the owner's head.

He tells me to tell the dishwasher not to show up the next day. He says that I should take over the dishwasher's duties. The dishwasher is startled by this order. He thinks that he's being fired. He asks why the owner is dissatisfied with his work. The owner has me assure him that the absence is only for a day.

The following day, peoples' moods are even more somber. Nobody says anything to me, and people talk to each other only in low voices. About eleven o'clock, the owner comes into the kitchen, and with a friendly manner, tells me to take a rest, to go home and not come back until four o'clock that afternoon. Deducing that the investigators from the labor office were due during that interval, I hang around near the restaurant, hoping to catch them on their way out. Hour after hour, from a seat in a hamburger stand not far away, I watch as people come and go from the restaurant. I consume a dozen soft drinks while I'm waiting, but I have no luck; I can't find a way to distinguish between the investigators and ordinary customers. The investigators come and go while I'm waiting, I'm sure, because when I return, everybody is happy. The owner, rubbing his hands together, tells me to resume working.

Going Home

THE SIMPSON-RODINO LAW

For several weeks, a news items has been drawing commentary, and inspiring either hope or worry, or both, in every wetback household. The news is about the promulgation of a law called Simpson-Rodino, whose object is to regularize Mexican immigration. Among its provisions is an amnesty for wets who have been in the United States since 1982 without having ever gone back home. People who qualify will be given residency, or "green cards." But first, they'll have to meet the documentary requirements. They'll have to go to the Immigration and Naturalization Service offices to apply, showing documents to prove that they've been here since 1982. And the law promises that they won't be deported for applying. Paycheck stubs, rent receipts, water, telephone or electric utility receipts, medical receipts and other consumer tallies can be used as proof. Once they've provided the INS with these documents, they will automatically be given permission to live and work in the United States, while action is taken on their applications. The news broadcasts talk about a deadline for applying and warn that the *Migra* may extend its nets when the deadline passes.

To guarantee that the new law measure be effective, the law also sets out rules for employers. Though workers hired before September, 1986 are exempt from the requirement, the law gives employers a deadline for verifying that all other workers are either citizens or legal immigrants, or that their amnesty papers have been filed. When the grace period ends, agents of *La Migra* will check business records. If undocumented workers are found on an employer's payroll, he will be subject to fines of from $250 to $10,000 for each wetback he employs.

While Spanish-language newspapers, television and radio stations, give almost daily bulletins about the new law, their announcements and advertising pages carry notices from a legion of lawyers that seem to have appeared from nowhere. The ads say things like, "We, your friends, lawyers So and So, can help you apply for amnesty. We promise you concern, professionalism and, above all, that information about your case will be kept in privacy. Visit us at our offices on Such-and-Such Street, or telephone us at such-and-such number."

Among my townsmen there is skepticism. They don't believe that the law will be enforced, either to benefit or to hurt them. "With a law like that, only a few of us can qualify," one of them tells me, "and if the government deports all the wetbacks, who will do our work? The restaurants hire us, the farmers hire us, we are the gardeners and the construction workers. The United States has a lot of machines and can do a lot of things, but it can't do without us yet."

A lot of townsmen, if not the majority of them, have been in the United States for longer than the law requires. But all of them have gone home to visit their families at least once a year, and almost no one has had any reason to save the stubs of his paychecks or his rent receipts. There are also lots of us who, like me, are paid in cash.

Before long, on the doors of restaurants and companies, signs appear that say, "We have no jobs for undocumented workers." But that's only a problem for the newly arrived, because the rest of us are exempt. Several employers even help their Mexican workers to procure documents saying that they've been here since 1982, and several of my townsmen who get the papers go to see a lawyer, who charges them three hundred dollars each. According to the grapevine, lately the city registry in our village has been deluged by requests for copies of birth certificates.

Several church groups have launched protests against the law, demanding that the authorities be more flexible in the requirements it sets for amnesty. They support their demands with humanitarian claims, because in some families, only one parent is eligible for amnesty. The Catholic church is asking if the government plans to split up families with its amnesty program. Little by little, the regulations announced at the outset are made more and more flexible, until at last, the INS agrees that if only one member of a family is eligible for amnesty, the whole family gets to stay. Farmers have also protested the law, saying that if it is strictly enforced, they'll have no field workers and will be quickly bankrupted. More concessions are made. The rules are changed so that wetbacks need present, not an uninterrupted series of rent receipts, for example, but only one receipt for each year. Another change allows an applicant who has no receipts to give an oral history of his stay in the United States. A board of examiners is created to decide on such cases.

Among all of this commotion, some employers take advantage of the ignorance of many wets regarding the new law, by paying them less than the minimum wage. For example, they tell their workers that by hiring them, "I'm exposing myself to a fine, and that means that I'll have to pay more to lawyers. If you want to work for me, you'll have to accept two dollars an hour."

Regardless of the law, wets keep arriving daily. In my village, the flow stopped only for a little while; within a few weeks, people started coming again, in the same numbers as always. My uncle Vicente, who is one of the few who has saved his check stubs, has applied for residency without hiring a lawyer. Some other relatives of mine who have been in the United States for less than two years have applied as well. They are now working in restaurants, with permits good for the next six months.

DECIDING

All considered, it *does* seem to be easier to qualify for residency under the new law, but I don't plan to try. Ever since the day in which I made my plans to come to the United States, it has been with the idea of earning dollars to change into pesos when I go back. Here in the United States, it's true that there are more comforts and luxuries, but not for people like dishwashers and busboys, whose earnings are meager.

Furthermore, life in the United States is completely a routine. Life is going to work, coming home and, on weekends and holidays, going to a movie or drinking beer. I suspect that to stay for the rest of my life would be to live a routine until my last days. In my village, it's not that way. We have festivals in which everybody practically lives together for three or four days at a time. That isn't to say that we are lazy, but instead, that we know how to work—and how to forget work for awhile.

Even if I could learn English, I couldn't integrate myself into American life because of the differences in customs, although in the U.S., customs do not exist so much as a way of life and laws for governing it. Even most of those townsmen who've been able to establish legal residency don't plan to stay in the United States for the rest of their lives. For example, my uncle Vicente, who has bought a house in Mexico, where his family lives. He visits them from time and time and plans to return to Mexico with machine-shop equipment to establish a business of his own. While he is working here, his children are in Mexican universities. Had he brought them, it is unlikely that they would have pursued higher education. What's more likely is that they would have fallen prey to drugs, and my uncle would have spent his last days like the old man in black gabardine that I knew in Houston. The few townsmen of mine who have raised their families in the United States go to great expense to send their children to the village during summers, so that the kids will not forget their roots.

I have more or less achieved the goals that impelled me to come

232

to the United States. I have sent some tools to the village, and I bought others to take when I go. I have also saved some dollars to help me settle comfortably. At first it was hard, but afterwards, it wasn't so bad. Now it is time for me to return to Mexico. If I should need to return here someday in the future, I will come back, but only for a short while.

I tell the owner of the restaurant that I'm working my last two-week pay period with him. As with Rolando, he tells me that if I come back, I can be sure of a job. He asks if I know of someone who can replace me, and I bring a townsmen to take my place. Before I go, some of my townsmen ask me to take money orders to their families, as I have done when others went home before me.

ALMOST HOME

A couple of big cardboard boxes are my baggage, more than I brought when I came. In addition to tools, I'm carrying clothing for my brothers, the kind that can be bought in Mexico, it's true, but only at exorbitant prices. Rolando takes me to the airport in his car, and there I board a Mexican airline for its red-eye flight to Mexico City.

On arriving in the morning in Mexico City, like all the passengers, I get in line for customs and immigration inspection, dragging my boxes behind me as the line moves. Everybody is nervous and is craning his neck to see how things are going for the passengers who are in line in front of them, facing the officials. "The agents go for electrical appliances, more than anything else," a woman ahead of me says. She says that she is bringing a television and a record player. To prepare for inspection, she puts some dollars in between the pages of her passport. That's her *mordida* or bribe money. "I hope they'll be content," she mutters from time to time. When her times comes, she smiles broadly at an agent who is eyeing her baggage.

"I'm not carrying any great things," she says. The agent remains silent and grave.

"What are you bringing?" he asks her, dryly.

"A television, but it is used."

"What else?"

"A record player, also second-hand."

"What more?"

"They're used, I've bought them second-hand."

"Open your baggage!" he says. "Move over there!"

"Look, here are my documents," the lady says, handing him the passport stuffed with bills.

I am the next in line. I don't offer the agents any money right away, but instead start untying the knots on my boxes.

"What is that you're bringing?" one of the agents asks me.

"Clothing and some tools."

I finish opening the box and the agent sticks his hands inside, running them along the sides of the box. Then he pulls out a bunch of clothing and looks down into the box, at my tools. After inspecting one box in this way, he goes to the other.

"Go on," he says, all of a sudden. I am surprised that he didn't ask me for money.

Before long, I reach the bus terminal. I buy my ticket for Oaxaca City, and am contentedly sitting in the waiting room when a man in street clothes spots me. In a minute, he is joined by four other men. They form a circle around me and one of them identifies himself as "the captain."

"We are federal agents and we're searching for arms. We're going to check your baggage," he says.

"I'm not carrying any guns," I tell them.

"Bring your boxes and we'll see," one of them says.

Obeying his orders, I carry my boxes into a hallway outside of the waiting room. The captain's helpers immediately begin untying my boxes. They toss the clothes to one side and begin taking out my tools, an electric sander, an electric saw, a manual typewriter, an electric router and other tools of lesser size.

"Where are you coming from?" they ask me, while taking more things out my boxes.

"I went as a wetback, I'm not carrying arms," I say.

The guy who claims to be a captain whistles softly, as if surprised.

"Oh, so you're a smuggler, uh? Put his things away and take him to the station wagon," he tells his assistants.

"I'm not a smuggler, captain. I went as a wetback, and in order to buy those tools, I had to work for a good bit of time. I'm no thief. I am a carpenter and I'm bringing these tools so that I can work with them myself."

"In any case, all of this is contraband," he answers, taking my saw out of the box. He points to a label on the saw that says, "Made in Japan."

"Isn't this contraband?" he asks.

"I don't want to resell it, I want it for work," I explain.

"We're going to have confiscate all of it," he threatens.

His helpers begin tying the ropes around the boxes again. When they've finished, they ask him if they shouldn't also take my boxes to the station wagon, so that they can process everything at once.

"You're evading import taxes," the captain tells me.

"Well, okay, you're right. I'll pay my taxes, but where should I pay them?"

"We'll have to take your things and then you'll have to go the Ministry to pay them. When you've paid, you can reclaim your things," he says.

I don't like the idea at all. It means that I'll lose sight of my boxes and I don't believe that if I do, I can be sure of ever seeing them again.

"Listen, captain, doesn't a guy have a right to earn a living? I went as a wetback, to work. It has cost me my own money to buy these tools."

The one who claims to be a captain looks at his helpers. Then he asks me how long I was in the United States, and what cities I visited, and where I'm headed now.

"I know that you've sweated to buy these things," the captain says, "but we're also here working, keeping watch, and if you think about it, you'll see that our work is also exhausting."

"But you already saw that I'm not bringing guns."

"Turn loose of something and we'll let you go," one of his assistants says. It's *mordida* time.

Before leaving Los Angeles, I had changed some dollars into pesos. I take out a twenty thousand peso bill and hand it to them, but they refuse it disdainfully.

"You'd better behave or we'll take your things," one of them threatens.

"Well, how much is enough, then?"

"At least another fifty thousand. We have to split it, you see."

"This is plain thievery," I think to myself. But to get away from the problem and to get my things out of danger, I begin counting.

I had thought myself safe from the need to pay bribes because I had been waiting for the customs agents at the airport to demand money, and they didn't. On the way to the bus station I'd been so happy, I had even decided to write a letter to my townsmen in Los Angeles, telling them about my good luck. But there's no point in that now; it seems, you not only have to have good luck in the airport, but also at the bus station.

I hand the extra money to the officials, and one of them puts it into his pocket. Without so much as saying thank you for the thousands that I've given them, they walk silently away, taking long paces with great dignity, as if instead of a robbery, they'd just carried out an act of justice.

That's the way Mexico works. It has always been that way. Back in *bracero* days my father paid *mordidas* to bring clothing with him, and my townsmen pay today. Everybody comes back ready to pay bribes, and the only real differences between individuals are that some have had to pay more than others, for no apparent reason. Faced with a *mordida* demand, you can't do anything but "turn loose of something." The authorities demand it, and they've got police identification in one hand and a pistol in the other. Besides, getting home with my tools is worth more than I had to pay. The inconveniences of a wetback's life last only until he gets home again.